THE
ACCOUNTABILITY
FACTOR

THE ACCOUNTABILITY FACTOR

How Implementing an Accountability System Boosts Employee Productivity and Company Profitability

OSWALD R. VIVA

Copyright © 2019 Oswald R. Viva.

All rights reserved. No part of this book may be used or reproduced by any means, graphic, electronic, or mechanical, including photocopying, recording, taping or by any information storage retrieval system without the written permission of the author except in the case of brief quotations embodied in critical articles and reviews.

Archway Publishing books may be ordered through booksellers or by contacting:

Archway Publishing
1663 Liberty Drive
Bloomington, IN 47403
www.archwaypublishing.com
1 (888) 242-5904

Because of the dynamic nature of the Internet, any web addresses or links contained in this book may have changed since publication and may no longer be valid. The views expressed in this work are solely those of the author and do not necessarily reflect the views of the publisher, and the publisher hereby disclaims any responsibility for them.

Any people depicted in stock imagery provided by Getty Images are models, and such images are being used for illustrative purposes only. Certain stock imagery © Getty Images.

ISBN: 978-1-4808-7790-0 (sc)
ISBN: 978-1-4808-7793-1 (hc)
ISBN: 978-1-4808-7791-7 (e)

Library of Congress Control Number: 2019908591

Print information available on the last page.

Archway Publishing rev. date: 6/28/2019

Also by Oswald R. Viva

Customizing VLSI IC Update: A User's Guide to the ASIC Design Center
Electronic Trends Publications. ISBN0-914405-16-0

**It's Lonely at the Top:
A Practical Guide to Becoming a Better Leader of Your Small Company**
iUniverse, Inc. ISBN-978-1-4620-4653-9;
ISBN-978-1-4620-4655-3; ISBN-978-1-4620-4654-6

Fundamentals of Job Interviewing for Managers
Amazon.com. ISBN-13 978-148022960; ISBN-10 1480222968

Performance Reviews: The Bad, the Ugly, the Alternative
Amazon.com. ISBN ISBN-13:978-1496144157; ISBN-10:1496144155

Accountability in the Workplace
www.SkillBites.net

You Are the Owner, But Are You the Right CEO?
www.SkillBites.net

Create a Culture of Empowerment
www.SkillBites.net

Delegate to Succeed
www.SkillBites.net

Exit Strategy and Succession Planning
www.SkillBites.net

A Compilation of My E-Books, 2012–2013
CreateSpace/Amazon.com
ISBN-13: 978-1497511996; ISBN-10: 1497511992

The Entrepreneurship Game: Can You Win at It?
CreateSpace/Amazon.com
ISBN-13: 978-1500520496; ISBN-10: 1500520497

**The Making of a CEO:
Helping You Deal with the Issues of Running Your Company**
CreateSpace/Amazon
ISBN - 978-1516942334; ISBN - 10-1516942531

FOREWORD

Former CEO, professional business consultant, CEO coach, mentor, teacher, writer, and leader, Oswald Viva has written this excellent book to help organizations, particularly business enterprises, implement accountability as a tool to improve performance. The awareness of the importance of accountability is critically pertinent and especially vital when we look at what is happening in our world today.

The insights and teachings within these pages can be applied personally, professionally, politically, and in our social and news media, our schools, and even our homes. There is a line that resonates with me: "Ambiguity is the enemy of accountability." Just take a moment, close your eyes, and picture the inaccuracies and vagueness we witness every day in our work lives, in our politicians, in our own homes with our children. What are our personal accountabilities that contribute to success and failure in those areas?

This book takes us from the parental role in raising a child to being accountable right to the board room. It provides thought-provoking and perceptive methods to drive companies toward creating an environment where accountability is encouraged and, in certain cases, even demanded.

Changing personal behavior is often a challenging task, but it can be accomplished with thoughtful dedication. Changing the culture of a company, especially a long-established company, is a daunting undertaking, requiring dedication, commitment, and endurance. This book is a guide that will not only start the process but explain how to implement a change in culture.

The book is written for and dedicated to a modern-day society craving accountability from its leaders in politics, business, education, and press and reporting agencies, in order to improve the performance of our businesses and our schools, the accuracy of information for public consumption, and the success of our country. Adopting a culture of accountability is a vehicle to guarantee the betterment of any organization.

Greatness begins with practicing accountability at all levels, with an impact on our lives and the lives of our children and future generations. This book teaches you how to implement it.

Deborah Vaughn
Manager, Hybrid Cloud Service Line
Client Technical Solution Services and Integrations
International Business Machines

To my family and extended family, whose love and support fuel my ambition to write.

CONTENTS

Introduction xiii

CHAPTER ONE 1
The Buck Stops Here
    Accountability versus Responsibility 3
    The Absence of Accountability 4

CHAPTER TWO 7
Societal Accountability
    Accountability in Society 7
    Accountability in Governance 8
    Accountability in the Media 11
    Accountability in Schools 13
    Accountability in the Home 16

CHAPTER THREE 19
Accountability in the Workplace
    The Work Environment 19
    Accountability and Delegation 27
    The Ladder of Accountability 36
    The Culture of Accountability 37

CHAPTER FOUR 41
Personal Accountability
    Self-Empowerment 49
    The Value of a Personal Accountability Plan 50

    Your Personal Accountability System 51
    Balancing Work and Life 62

CHAPTER FIVE 69
Accountability and Leadership
    Clarity Is Key and Starts with You 79
    Team Accountability 80

CHAPTER SIX 87
Implementation
    The Process of Implementation 87
    Barriers to Implementing Accountability 95
    Removing the Barriers 96
    Implementing Accountability in Your Organization 98
    The Difficult Part: How to Correct a Lack of Accountability ... 102

CHAPTER SEVEN 109
Other Cases of Accountability
    How to Evaluate Remote Employees 109
    Perfecting Performance Reviews 112

CHAPTER EIGHT 115
Epilogue
    Summary 116
    Ten Truths of Personal Accountability 117

Bibliography 119

APPENDIX A 121
What Is Accountability?

APPENDIX B 123
Making People Accountable

APPENDIX C 127
Delegation

INTRODUCTION

This book highlights a serious problem prevalent in our society today, from the home to the workspace, from the school to the media, and not forgetting the government. Somehow, personal accountability and organizational accountability are seriously lacking in our world. Accountability boils down to taking ownership of one's own thoughts, words, actions, and reactions. Without personal accountability, there is no organizational accountability, and without that, businesses and organizations fail to reach their ultimate potential.

When accountability is prevalent in an organization, employees stop blaming each other, departments stop shifting the blame to other departments, retailers see their own weaknesses instead of blaming the competition, everyone stops blaming the government for all their pains, and the organization gains in productivity, well-being, and total richness.

Accountability means a commitment to meet or exceed agreed-to expectations while admitting mistakes and errors. Accountable people accept the consequences of the choices they make; they do what's right just because it's the right thing to do. It is really a cultural value that requires all team members to assume responsibility for their own and each other's actions and to focus on the actions required at the individual and team level to improve everyone's performance and therefore increase the performance of the organization.

There is probably nothing more important to effective management than a clearly defined, integrated set of processes. Defined to fit the actual work environment, clear processes effectively utilize all resources: human, mechanical, and financial, but if the people in the organization fail to implement those processes or fail to own the responsibility for accuracy and truth in their implementation, the processes fail the organization and its people.

Accountability systems are designed to instill discipline into a process, that is, produce the ability to consistently repeat good practices. Processes must be maintained, and a system of accountability provides the checks and balances to keep the process running. From top to bottom, from the CEO to the last employee on the organization chart, being accountable, both at work and away from work, is a cultural application that, once instilled, will improve productivity and build returns on investment tenfold.

To help groups and individuals work in ways that promote the desired outcomes, measures are developed to give feedback on how well or poorly that work is accomplishing the goals. Accountability is the best and most efficient way to instill organization-wide performance that keeps everyone on the same playing field. Accountability ensures that, despite the complexity of the work and the context in which it exists, individuals, groups, and, ultimately, the organization as a whole will understand their part in accomplishing the goals.

Accountability starts with the leader and must travel throughout the whole organization. Whether your organization embraces a culture of accountability or is in need of a reboot in this department, it all begins and ends with the leaders. Without full and unabated implementation of a cultural mind-set of accountability, it will not only fail; it will be worse than it was before.

We discuss why accountability is needed and how enterprises and their people benefit from creating a culture of accountability. Learn what it really means to have an organizational culture of accountability and see how to implement it in your business. It's not a dirty word; it's not a militaristic way of life. It's not a discipline-driven culture. It's one that sets the bar and signals to people that high performance is expected, recognized, and rewarded.

In these pages, we briefly discuss the lack of accountability in society in general, but we emphasize the work environment. We believe it is important to mention the impact of accountability—or the lack of it—in politics, schools, the media, and the home because it is a cancer that affects society in general. This cancer propagates into most areas of our lives and even into the business sector which is the main target of this book.

I'm a staunch promoter of accountability in society in general and in business in particular; my clients know how important the practice is for me and for them because I instill it in them. Some of them call me "Mr. Accountability," and they gratefully acknowledge my help in making them accountable.

Ambiguity is the enemy of accountability. Be certain in what you do, and accept failure as an accident, but don't accept ineptitude as a condition.

CHAPTER ONE
THE BUCK STOPS HERE

Why accountability? What is it, and why there is so much talk about it? Leaders claim they need it as an indispensable piece of any organization, but do they really know what it is and how to use it? Shareholders demand it but don't enforce it. Why do employees fear it? Why do we claim it is lacking in our society?

In leadership roles, accountability is acknowledging and assuming responsibility for actions, products, decisions, and policies, encompassing the obligation to report situations, explain decisions, and be answerable for resulting consequences. It is a guiding principle that defines the working fundamentals of everything and every activity in an organization. It is the nerve center that controls every part of an organization and affects all members and their relationships with each other.

Accountability is the obligation of an individual or organization to account for its activities, accept responsibility for them, and disclose the results in a transparent manner. It also includes responsibility for money and other entrusted property. Sadly, personal accountability is severely lacking in business and across society in general. For example, some businesses falsify financial or productivity reports to mislead the market about their true financial status.

To be accountable means to commit to a specific course of action or outcome, within a defined time frame and other metrics, and being obliged to accomplish it. A commitment involves a promise, and not achieving it involves failing to keep one's word. A promise is like a contract, and failing to deliver is defaulting on the contract. Other people counting on this outcome should receive an account of the responsible person's performance. When you give your word, you have an obligation to alert others if it appears that you won't meet the target; others have the right to expect advance notice.

It follows, then, that accountability has two components: Someone is responsible for something, and someone else makes sure that person accomplishes what he or she committed to within the parameters established. The parameters may include quality, time, cost, and others as proposed by the person assigning the job and accepted by the one doing the work. Most commonly, what fails is the first component—people not assuming responsibility—but it is even more damaging when the second component fails, when managers or supervisors don't enforce accountability or even ignore the need for it.

Some failures may be acceptable if the responsible person takes a normal course of action with the right rationale, facts, and effective communication of issues. Accountability also can be recognized if early detection of failures, appropriate communication, and damage reparation are promptly implemented. Responsible behavior can lessen the negative impact of failures.

Accountability involves commitments, promises, obligations, rights, and consequences.

Consequences for success are easy and can take the form of
- praise,
- gratitude,
- recognition,
- rewards,
- celebrations,
- promotions,
- bonuses or raises,
- increased responsibilities, and
- freedom to act.

Consequences of failures are more difficult; they involve
- team disappointments,
- recognition that those responsible let their team down,
- tough conversations or postmortems,
- failure to get rewards,
- erosion of trust,
- limitations on opportunities for advancement or desirable assignments, and
- possibly discipline or even termination.

Accountability is one of the key elements of leadership and a skill set that everyone can learn. We are all responsible for our own success. The ability to deliver optimum results in any organization is directly related to the accountability attitudes, practices, and systems that are in place; if accountability is not working, it negates all efforts toward performance improvements. In the business world, accountability cannot exist without proper accounting practices. Since you can't manage what you don't measure, an absence of accounting means an absence of accountability.

Accountability versus Responsibility

Accountability and *responsibility* are two words that are often used as synonyms but in reality are very different in meaning. Dictionaries give different meanings to each of these words, and in practice, the difference is even more distinct.

Webster's definitions:

> Accountability: the quality or state of being accountable; especially: an obligation or willingness to accept responsibility and to account for one's actions.
>
> Accountable: subject to giving an account, as in "held her *accountable* for the damage."

> Responsibility: The state or fact of being responsible, answerable, or accountable for something within one's power, control, or management.
>
> Responsible: liable to be called to account as the primary cause, motive, or agent.

In practice, the main difference between responsibility and accountability is that responsibility can be shared, while accountability cannot. Being accountable for something not only means having assigned the responsibility but also being answerable for one's actions. When accountability is prevalent in an organization, employees stop blaming each other, departments stop shifting the blame to other departments, retailers see their weaknesses instead of blaming the competition, everyone stops blaming the government for all their pains, and the organization gains in productivity, well-being, and total richness.

Problems occur when an organization doesn't achieve the results desired and searches for culprits. That's when those responsible for a job are identified and blamed. But those accountable for the failure need to be identified too. Regretfully, the two words are not always used properly. Responsibility is assigned, as in "you are responsible for painting that window," while accountability is taking ownership to achieve the necessary results—to see it to completion, to own it, to solve any deficiency, and to meet the specifications of the job. You can be *given* responsibility, but you have to *take on* accountability.

The Absence of Accountability

How many times has your company missed a shipment, deadline, or goal because someone did not follow through on a commitment? I'm sure this has happened more times than you care to admit. How many times has the company received complaints from customers because someone didn't provide the service they expected? Think about how strong your company's commitment is to accountability and efforts to provide a culture of accountability; it could be better, right? Now is the time to change that and get it right.

Pointing fingers, blaming, or using excuses to justify a failure only guarantees that problems will repeat themselves. My guess is that you've heard people say, "I did my part," or "I didn't have the right tools," or "I just followed instructions," or "John didn't give me the right spec." You get the idea. All those reasons are mere excuses that have no place in a well-run organization. They are typical of an organization that lacks accountability, where there is a sense that "good enough" or "close to the spec" is acceptable or that the specs are not important or silly. I like to say, "If it's good enough, it ain't." These issues are also prevalent in organizations with an internal focus rather than a client focus.

Of course, the problem has a negative impact on productivity, quality, the number of clients, revenue, profits, and organizational morale. Of all those negatives, the most important is the effect on the morale of the people; all others are easier to recover from than morale. Generally speaking, employees want to excel; they want to be proud of their performance—whether it is for self-satisfaction or just to stay out of trouble—but they also want to be liked by coworkers and avoid conflicts.

Introducing accountability can feel uncomfortable in the short term; employees will resent the idea as a measure by management to tighten the reins and identify culprits of bad performance. They are probably used to the practice that when things go smoothly, nobody asks who is responsible for the success; it is only when there are problems that management wants to know who screwed up. This will not help the company's cause to create the right culture.

My Experience

I consulted for a start-up that had a great promising product, an advanced technology in the consumer's marketplace with extraordinary applications. The founders invested a substantial amount of money; hired several engineers and vice presidents of sales, engineering, and production; and traveled to the Far East to woo potential investors. All this was done with the expectations that investors would flock in, attracted by the product. Unfortunately, the technology was not as ready as promoted, and it became obvious when the prototypes were demonstrated. In addition, the supposedly nascent market was not as ready as they thought, and there were doubts as to its eventual readiness.

After unsuccessfully courting VCs and individual investors, money ran out, and the entrepreneurs were forced to close the business, resulting in a major financial loss, pink slips for everyone hired in the enthusiastic mood, and even some lawsuits for breach of contract. If the developers of the technology had been honest about its status, and if the engineers had evaluated it consciously, and if the principals had done a true analysis of the market rather than looking at it with embellished eyes, they could have prevented all this pain.

This, of course, was sadly a perfect example of lack of accountability all around. The engineers were not accountable to their function regarding the readiness of the technology. Management was not accountable to hold engineers accountable, and the principals were not accountable to all stakeholders because they did not hold their end of the project regarding the availability of the market. In this case, lack of accountability had a drastic effect, with many people paying the consequences.

Takeaways from Chapter 1

- To be accountable means to commit to a specific course of action or outcome.
- Accountability has two components: people are responsible for something, and someone else makes sure they accomplish what they committed to, within the parameters established.
- Accountability involves commitments, promises, obligations, rights, and consequences.
- Accountability is one of the key elements of leadership and a skill set that everyone can learn.
- Lack of accountability has a negative impact on productivity and quality.

CHAPTER TWO
SOCIETAL ACCOUNTABILITY

Accountability in Society

One of the biggest problems that we have in our society today is a lack of personal accountability. Nobody is ever wrong, and when they do make mistakes, there is always an excuse. In today's world, lack of accountability is prevalent in most parts of society, including government, schools, work, and family. Any organization that has faced a problem with missed deadlines, productivity shortfalls, quality issues, poor follow-up, or customer complaints surely can trace their source to lack of accountability by someone or some group.

Embarking on projects without clear performance objectives or assigning owners to tasks is a common mistake that can cause the collapse of expectations. These breakdowns typically result in finger-pointing, searching for culprits, and general unhappiness and personal discomfort within the organization.

When parents clean their child's room because they are tired of seeing a mess, when managers step in to complete a task that an employee was supposed to do because it needs to be finished now, they are not teaching responsibility and are not providing lasting value. Obviously, then, they are refraining from teaching accountability by not holding accountable those responsible for completing the tasks they were assigned. Defining responsibility boundaries is a critical step in the process of embracing accountability. Clarifying who is responsible for what and how that responsibility is assigned and measured are critical steps.

Many people expect, and even demand, handouts from the government, in many cases not out of necessity but just because if the help is there for the taking, why not take advantage of it? This is an obvious lack of responsibility and ultimately of accountability because those people rely on handouts rather than assuming responsibility for their lives. Without responsibility, there can be no accountability. This issue falls to the government because it allows this to happen by not demanding (or even asking) people to assume their obligations as citizens.

According to a survey by the American Management Association, a large portion of business leaders admit that 30 to 50 percent of employees aren't held accountable for their performance. Accountability is not a new concept, and the requirements for it have been around a long time. Precepts that have long been known include communicate clear expectations; align individual and team goals with departmental and organizational strategies and vision; provide time, training, tools, and resources; empower people to succeed; provide recognition and feedback; and take action when individuals and teams do not meet expectations.

Many blame this behavior on worker problems, in that the employees do not follow instructions and are not interested in being accountable, but the problem is more serious than that. Lack of accountability transmits to all facets of life; if people are used to and feel comfortable not producing and getting their needs satisfied without any effort from their part, it is also difficult for them to be responsible and accountable at work or at school. Workers who act that way don't own their jobs, they rent them; without ownership, there is no responsibility or accountability.

Accountability in Governance

Government officials, civil servants, and everyone in a position to serve the public have a duty to act visibly and predictably to promote participation of the public and be measured with the corresponding accountability. In a democracy, the principle of accountability calls for government officials to be responsible to the citizenry for their decisions and the resulting actions. Also required is transparency; decisions are to be open to public scrutiny, and the public should have access to the process. Transparency and accountability together enable citizens to have a say about the issues that matter to them; they have the opportunity to influence their decisions and hold those making the decisions to account.

Political accountability refers to the responsibility and obligation of public officials to act in the best interest of the people they serve, the citizenship, directly or through legislative bodies such as Congress. Public officials should be held responsible for their actions or face consequences. Legal accountability concerns the mechanisms by which public officials can be held liable for actions that go against established rules. There are independent units formed to scrutinize and hold departments accountable; *independent* is the key word, as they are built on independence to avoid any conflict of interest. Nice words, good policies, but lacking in practice.

Accountability is desired and necessary in all phases of life, but in many cases, this desire is no more than a dream. We know very well that accountability in government is seriously lacking; sadly, we have examples of it every day, and it happens (or, better yet, it doesn't happen) in all levels of government: national, state, regional, and local. But why is this deficiency so prevalent? In private organizations, accountability is typically direct, meaning from an employee or team to a supervisor or management. In the public sector (government), accountability is from elected or unelected officials to the citizens, and the only feedback from citizens to government officials is by means of the vote. Politics gets involved in all cases and distorts the essential part of accountability, which is communications.

Because of politics, government officials have many ways to mask communications to the citizens, who use the vote to help those they like for whatever reason—party affiliation, dislike of the opponents, selfishness, and so on—disregarding any possible accountability measure. Ideally, government accountability is obtained through the use of political, legal, and administrative means, designed to prevent corruption and ensure that public officials assume responsibility to respond to the people they serve. Without those mechanisms, corruption may thrive, but those same mechanisms are used by politicians to distort or mask their performance. This is very unfortunate, but it is a sad reality.

Also because of the above, how accountable public officials are depends to a large extent on whether they are elected or appointed and, if elected, how many terms they can serve and when they are up for reelection. Since the US Congress doesn't have term limits, many senators and representatives serve in their positions for many years (some for decades), and thus, they discount accountability. It is difficult to hold them accountable. Regardless of how they serve, legal accountability measures include the Constitution, legislative acts, rules and codes, and other instruments that proscribe what officials can and cannot do, how they should be accountable to the citizens, and what these can do to ensure accountability. In theory, this should be the guarantor of government accountability, but in practice, it is not sufficient. Personal accountability should be the practice, but in many (most?) cases, it doesn't exist.

It is also true that too many measures to ensure accountability prevent organizations from achieving their mission. Greiling and Halachmi, in "Transparency, E-Government, and Accountability," published in *Public Performance & Management Review* in 2013, claim that in the real world, where the proverbial question is "Why can't government be like business?" many public managers are challenged by the need to perform a balancing act between the pursuit of greater openness and private-sector efficiency. The article concludes that there is a need to develop theories, models, and trainings to assist managers in addressing this balancing challenge. They also tell us that "accountability has to do with appropriateness of actions and adherence to obligations." They propose "designing proper and adequate accountability arrangements to foster organizational learning" as a new goal for accountability. They argue that measuring actual performance by individuals or organizations is a better approach to improve results than merely finding mistakes and pointing accusatory fingers, which we corroborate in this book as a key to accountability.

Aside from voting in regular elections, recall elections can be used to revoke the office of an elected official. Impeachment is another penalty imposed to remove officials from their post; however, this measure is reserved to the Congress and not available to the public. Generally, though, the public does not have any direct way to hold elected officials accountable during the term for which they have been elected. In addition, because many different individuals in a large public organization contribute to its performance, it is difficult to identify who should be accountable for poor results. If individuals, or even teams or groups of individuals, who could not have prevented the results are held accountable and unfairly punished, the real culprits go free, and the weakness of the organization is not identified and corrected. Thus, the main goal of politicians is to get votes regardless of how they are gained, disregarding any accountability measures.

Accountability in the Media

The media is a complex system that changes with time, politics, technology, history, and political orientation of those in government and in the media itself. For good or for bad, it is obvious that the media plays an important role in a country's development. It is the nexus between the public and the governing forces and, as such, is subjected to individual sentiments and whatever message the government wants to transmit and the media wants to report. The media can transmit citizens' voices, but it can also change them to fit its sentiments toward a party, a policy, or certain people. It claims that it reports what the people are thinking, but many times, it inserts its own angle to accommodate whatever message it wants to send.

Traditional media accountability is under pressure because of the technological changes in the industry and the new methods by which people receive and disseminate information. In the traditional media, accountability resides in a code of practice that's agreed to but not always adhered to and investigation of complaints from the public. The acceptable practice of accountability in traditional media consisted of only reporting information received from two verified sources. The new media, using technology and what is commonly known as social media, is not governed by that practice; instead, it's driven by individual desires and only controlled by codes of decency and the morality of the media outlet providers.

There is no accountability in the online world, and the tone of journalism is different; there is more partisanship and more directly attached to people's feelings. Today's media accountability is practically reduced to tweets. News sources are not validated before they are aired; instead, they carry opinions and judgments. What we call news media today can be compared to Hollywood gossip publications. This may sound crude and too critical, but it is, in most cases, the reality of today's world.

Journalists can strengthen their own position by doing a better job of holding themselves accountable and showing more transparency in their work. There is an open debate regarding the need for greater professionalism and transparency in journalism. The availability and growth of unprofessional and unaccountable information drives disconformity from the public about the role of the media in society and is one of the reasons for the decline in readership of most media outlets. The issue of media accountability must be considered in its proper context in this complex era of the media being ever more powerful in the information age.

The fragmentation of both old and new media is producing separate and parallel worlds of information, which can reinforce prejudice and help the hand of those who use this division to consolidate their power. Understanding power also means understanding the role of media in accountability; party allegiance heavily influences the message in traditional media. People and states may see the world through the eyes of the law, but politicians see it through the eyes of the media, and the traditional media transmits the message that their side of politics wants people to see.

For accountability to exist in journalism, it falls to individuals in the industry to be open about what it stands for. Everyone needs to understand that freedom of information is not a media privilege but a key part of what freedom in general is based on. Transparency and accountability need to be joined by a growth in explanation and context. The public must demand good work, but it must also believe in the necessity of it and in the need for accountability. There are some sources invested in the need for accountability in accuracy of what is reported; one such source is FactCheck.org.

Making themselves accountable, owning up to their mistakes, and revealing their weaknesses is not something journalist do very well. They can attack politicians and popular personalities, and they love to dish out punishment, but they are notoriously shy when it comes to admitting their own flaws. This failure of the media to be open and accept accountability is seen by the general public as a symptom of arrogance and complacency. Media accountability, in whatever form it takes place, must be based upon the concept of self-ruling, but to be credible, these self-ruling commissions must be completely independent from regular media and must provide the opportunity to complain to those affected by inaccuracy of the reports.

To summarize, then, self-accountability in the media rarely exists; it will most likely continue to be missing for all practical purposes. It would be great for the country if the media, particularly what's known as the mainstream media, implemented even a modest measure of accountability. It would diminish, among other benefits, the ugly divisions that exist among people today. And it is the people who have the power to move the media into accountability by promoting and using only those outlets that believe in it.

Accountability in Schools

Educational systems use various ways of accountability; in general, they all concern performance of students. In some cases, the school is held responsible for the performance of its students, while in others, the teachers and administrators are the responsible parties. Systems in which schools or individual personnel are held responsible for aspects of the educational process are generally used to adjust the process of education. Regardless of who is assigned the responsibility, the educational accountability approach is termed "system accountability."

To have a workable accountability system, there must be a goal to aim at and measurements to utilize in pursuit of the goal, as well as criteria to be used to determine if the goal was met or to assess why it was not. Accountability in schools is generally measured by evaluating student performance. School accountability has become a key element of government education policies, and legislators use it to determine the incentives that schools receive to raise student achievement in the main subjects. It can also affect which students receive the most attention. Accountability systems have two basic elements: academic standards and standardized tests to measure individual performance. Standardized tests are sometimes used to group students in separate academic tracks, determine eligibility for promotion, and award funds to schools, teachers, or students.

School accountability can have different consequences. One approach is to include explicit rewards for performance that exceeds expectations. The rewards can include increased resources allocated to the school or autonomy to use those resources as the school prefers. It can also include bonuses for educators who have contributed to the success of the school. Since accountability by definition includes consequences, legislators may impose sanctions on those schools not meeting expectations. These sanctions may include removal of autonomy, requiring education agencies to provide additional schooling options to the schools, and, in an extreme case, outright school closure.

Individual student accountability is typically measured via examinations. The requirement is for students to pass tests that demonstrate they are ready to move up to a higher grade or leave the system with a certificate of successful completion of the requirements. The criteria used to show that the goal was met include a passing score on the test. Individual accountability for teachers and administrators includes various methods, such as teachers passing a test to keep their jobs or administrators receiving bonuses based on student achievement. They also include, as with any accountability system, criteria for determining consequences for failure.

School districts issue report cards for all their schools; these reports are useful to parents for selecting a school for their children. Accountability reports are generated to comply with federal legislation that requires annual report cards on the educational progress of schools and school districts. They contain data (indicators) designed to inform parents and the general public about the progress of public schools. These reports provide certain additional information of interest on the status of the district's schools and serve as accountability reports.

Student accountability is traditionally based on having rules and sanctions for infringement, but one type of school uses a different system. A Sudbury school is a type of school, usually for the K–12 age range, where students have complete responsibility for their own education; the school is run by direct democracy in which students and staff are almost equals. Students independently decide what to do with their time and tend to learn as a by-product of ordinary experience rather than through coursework. There is no predetermined educational syllabus, prescriptive curriculum, or standardized instruction. This is a democratic form of education. In this system, everyone (adults and students) are treated equally, and there is no authority other than that granted by the students.

The intended culture within a Sudbury school includes freedom, trust, respect, responsibility, and democracy. They are based on the belief that children are extremely good at (and therefore do not need to be taught) the main behaviors they will need as adults, including responsibility and judgment, and that freedom is essential to the development of personal responsibility. Students are given responsibility for their own education. They design what they will learn; there are no tests or evaluations. Parents have very limited involvement.

So then, how is accountability applied? Because students are given the sole responsibility, they own their work and are accountable for their accomplishment, but who are they accountable to? Primarily to themselves and secondarily to their peers, students just like them who will suffer consequences from not learning from the students who do not achieve what they are supposed to achieve. Sudbury schools are not unique, as there are other schools practicing similar cultures.

Most of the comments above are for elementary, primary, and secondary education schools, as they are commonly known, and for college- or university-level public schools. For private schools and universities, the process and rules of accountability are different because the government doesn't play a role in them; for the most part, they are mandated by their own set of rules. Schools do much for our children, but they could do much more if accountability were directly and fairly applied to student progress.

Accountability in the Home

In the next chapter, we discuss how everyone in the organization must be held accountable if we are to create a culture of accountability. We also state that accountability starts at the top; whoever is at the top must set the example. It is the same in the home; the leader (father, mother, or whoever has that role) must set an example and be the first to assume responsibility and accountability. Children are not born with responsibilities, and everything they do is by instinct, so it follows that they must be taught responsibility and the corresponding step, which is accountability. However, parents don't always promote accountability, and that is a problem in many homes.

The age of accountability is not a rule that applies to all children; it depends on a number of circumstances and conditions, such as the environment in the home, a child's personality and ability to assume responsibilities, the teaching of accountability by the parents, and the willingness of the parents to delegate responsibility to the children. If children are old enough to be responsible, they are also old enough to be accountable, at least to the level of their responsibilities. Parents have to hold children accountable for not meeting their responsibilities, but first, they have to teach them responsibility. Of course, the methods used, the responsibilities assigned, and the penalties and rewards used are fully dependent on the age of the children. The rewards have to motivate children to accept their responsibilities and therefore assume the consequences—good or bad. Being held accountable requires parents to enforce the consequences for not meeting responsibilities, which are less pleasant than if children meet those responsibilities, and this in turn promotes a willingness to meet responsibilities in the future.

To teach children responsibility, start the process as early as possible (obviously considering the ages of the children). If you have assigned responsibilities, don't do those things for them; instead, help them while teaching what responsibility means. Use a language of encouragement as opposed to criticizing, and connect rewards with the responsibility. Be an example by consistently meeting your own responsibilities. Explain what your responsibilities are and how to meet them, and make it clear for them to see it happening. Teach and coach responsibility by explaining that responsibilities are commitments and that other people depend on you meeting those commitments. When children develop personal responsibility, they avoid many of the pitfalls of life they will face as grown-ups.

Be present in the life of your children at all times. Accountability requires a constant teaching practice, not only when a child makes a mistake. Create an environment at home conducive to teaching. Don't talk down to children; give them the freedom to respond respectfully instead of forcing them to lie to get out of uncomfortable situations. Coach them to admit their mistakes and give them the chance to make amends. For older children, let them say what they see as an appropriate consequence of their mistake and follow through with their choice of consequences.

Helping children become accountable has implications for their future because accountable children become accountable adults who have a brighter future in their personal and professional lives. Your efforts affect your children's entire life, so act accordingly.

It is not my intent here to teach parents what to do, as that is for each parent to decide what is best for them and for their children. I just propose actions based on the subject we discuss here.

There are many articles regarding parenting and accountability available in the literature, so we will not expand on this subject, as it is not the main purpose of this book.

CHAPTER THREE

ACCOUNTABILITY IN THE WORKPLACE

The Work Environment

Creating an environment where even modest accountability is fostered isn't easy, but unfortunately, many organizations make it harder than it needs to be. What is required is a system that empowers people to be more responsible and accountable, without resorting to punitive measures. It isn't about finding fault, blaming, or focusing on should-haves; it's about seeing the best in and expecting the best from those we interact with. In fact, when done properly, holding others accountable can actually build stronger relationships.

Many organizations spend significant time and resources but fail to develop people willing to work through difficult obstacles to meet goals and resolve problems; instead of looking for their root causes, they look for culprits and spread blame. But these attempts fail because accountability is looked at in punitive terms; people see synonyms of blame, fault, and one-sided measures imposed by management rather than responsibility, self-empowerment, and personal ownership of results. Organization mandates usually are not motivators for change; change only happens when individuals are motivated from within to see what's in it for them in the accountability game and are given the resources to apply a new behavior on the job.

The motivators for this new behavior are the recognition that success or failure of their job is up to them and not dependent on others or on circumstances outside of their control; accountability is owned by everyone in the organization, including management. Recognition by management of subordinates' success augments the motivation and thus welcomes self-accountability. Job satisfaction improves, stress goes down, and performance improves significantly. Praise in public, and praise often.

If leaders don't hold everyone—including themselves—accountable for outstanding performance, they compromise their organization, reduce their work section, and diminish their own credibility. People want to see others held accountable, and that includes all members of the organization. Everyone is accountable for their own behavior; leaders at all levels are ultimately responsible for their subordinates' performance, and as such, they should be held accountable too. By setting their own standards of exceptional performance, managers teach employees to accept accountability for their own actions and attitudes. And those leaders who own up to their mistakes as well as successes and accept the responsibility for their failures become allies in the process.

My Experience

The start-up I joined when I left IBM was not a typical small business; rather, it was more like a large VC-backed company. It was cash-rich, thanks to plenty of cash from investors who believed in the company. Nevertheless, it serves to illustrate my points above regarding leaders holding themselves accountable and holding their subordinates accountable as well.

When I reported to work as a founding member, responsible for a good part of the operations, I was told by the chairman that I had x amount of dollars to spend on the piece of the company under my direction. I told him I did not need that much; as a start-up, I thought we needed to be frugal. For example, we could lease equipment instead of buying it. I was told that the amount had been reserved for that purpose, and thus, I should go ahead and spend it.

Spending is easy, so I did that. The same philosophy was employed with the rest of the company; consequently, we drained large amounts of cash. The error of this mandate was experienced when—for a number of reasons that are not relevant here—we exhausted the capital and eventually went into bankruptcy. Had we been more conscious of expenditures, holding management and employees accountable and conserving cash, perhaps we could have avoided the bankruptcy phantom.

The competitive climate in all types of organizations eliminates the degrees of accountability traditionally imposed by job title or position. All employees, not just management, have to step up and be more accountable for their personal results and for the organization's results. I always recommend creating a functional organization chart, replacing or supplementing the classical positional and titles chart, and including the accountability levels of every function. When ownership (responsibility) is spelled out in the functional organization chart, time and energy are saved, and members feel more informed. Everyone who participates in a project becomes fully accountable for its success; leaders don't assume all the responsibility. For this reason, there is a tendency to replace—or supplement—traditional organizational charts with accountability charts that provide clarity about who owns the major functions of an organization and identify the primary roles and responsibilities for which they are accountable.

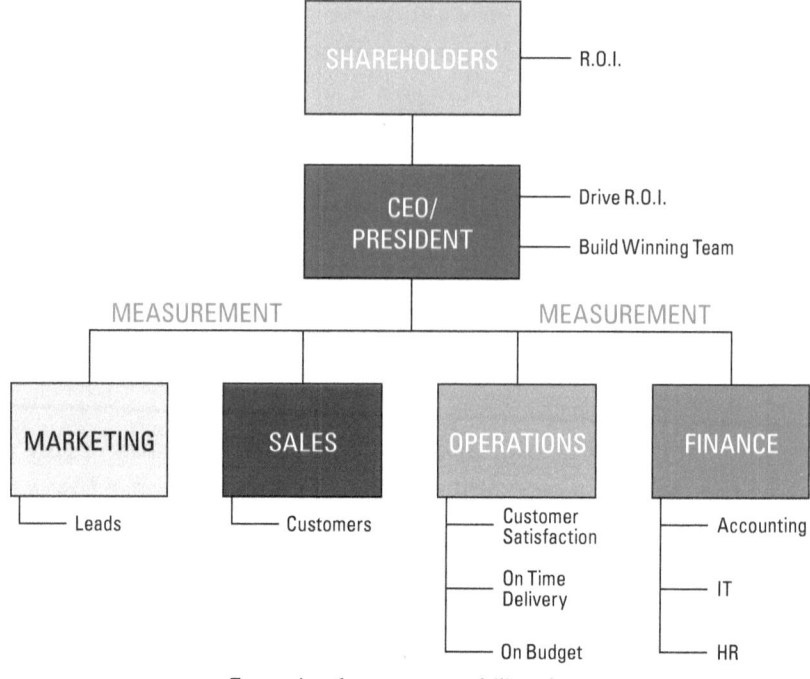

Example of an accountability chart.

In this chart, the CEO/president drives the return on investment (ROI) expected by the shareholders. Each department is accountable for its responsibilities, and results are measured to define its accountability.

Clarifying accountability improves the efficiency of an organization and eliminates some of the issues that affect it. Is it clear for the team who is responsible for what? Are goals not accomplished because nobody is driving them? It is important in every organization to clarify this accountability; whether there is an important problem or a minor one, time and energy are saved if members don't have to guess who owns the problem. How much time is wasted because of this accountability knowledge gap? This is not only a requirement for those at the top but for every level in the organization, regardless of the importance of the tasks. There should be only one owner for all major responsibilities, and everyone should understand who owns what.

Organizational charts are focused on hierarchical positions and who reports to whom, but they don't address a key issue in any organization: They lack clarity about who is accountable for what. Adding accountability to the typical organization chart explains who occupies the primary roles and the responsibilities for which they are accountable. It is very important to make it clear and universally understood who owns the responsibility for each function and thus who is accountable for what.

My Experience

A former client and friend hired a knowledgeable engineer expert in the core business of the company as a key member of the start-up. To convince him to take the risk of joining a new venture, my friend gave him the title of vice president of engineering. As the company grew and became a successful enterprise, it became obvious that the engineer did not have the capability to operate as a high-level executive.

My friend could not release him because his engineering talents were too valuable to give up, but he faced a conundrum to keep him motivated and also build the organization for the long term. When he made the hiring mistake, he did not think about accountability. Finally, upon my advice and my push to hold him accountable, the VP title was changed to chief technical officer, without any managerial responsibilities. The engineer was happy with his new title, and my friend was able to continue to build the organization without the wrongly placed person. Accountability counts in all phases of business, even in unexpected instances.

In project management, it is common to use a responsibility assignment matrix to identify the roles of various members of a project team. This matrix consists of a structural chart that makes clear what should be done by whom. It makes clear what the tasks and responsibilities are of each of the team members. It is also referred to as a RACI (Responsibility, Accountability, Consulted, and Informed) matrix, a VERI matrix, or an LRC (Linear Responsibility Chart).

Putting the responsibility assignment matrix in writing helps identify any mistakes or problems. Moreover, the participants in the project will have a better understanding of what their participation requires. It is especially useful in clarifying roles and responsibilities in cross-functional or complex projects and processes.

All leaders of companies strive for a workforce that embraces accountability, and they should demonstrate it by their actions. It is easy to claim accountability when results are positive, but when situations are less than favorable, it is more difficult to claim full responsibility. Business leaders—at least leaders of small and medium-size companies—want to be held accountable. In my work as CEO coach, I found that owners of small and midsize businesses enjoyed being members of leadership boards, where peers (and a coach) held them accountable for their performance. By their own admission, a major reason for joining those boards was to have accountability.

Part of my job as coach was to help them define the course of their businesses and guide them in its accomplishment. Whether reviewing steps of their strategic plan or simply critiquing actions to be implemented, confirming the results, positive or negative, was an important part of the coaching. They encouraged this role and welcomed the critique of their peers and myself. They admitted that this process helped them achieve what their companies needed. Of course, they also implemented the accountability system throughout their organizations, using what they learned by being themselves accountable.

For example, I asked business leaders (owners and CEOs) to develop targets (goals) for quarterly and yearly performance of their businesses, and the board of peers and myself judged their accomplishments against those goals. We as a group held them accountable, and the consequences of not meeting the goals were exposing their failure to their peers and setting more stringent goals for the next period. As proud business owners and leaders, they strived hard to meet their goals and prevent the consequences, resulting in marked improvements in the performance of their business. For other executives, I had them develop shorter goals (monthly, semimonthly, or even weekly, in some cases) based on their personal performance and its effect on the performance of the business. All of them (owners and nonowners) found these exercises extremely valuable and rewarding. (Appendix C shows some sample exercises.)

What are the elements of accountability?

- A system for budget management that includes what reports are needed, in what format and at what periods, and what actions must be addressed.
- A system to define the frequency and content of meetings, how they should be structured, what should be discussed.
- A system that identifies problems early, prioritizes them, gets the right people involved, generates a set of possible solutions, and tracks the success of the solution once it is implemented.
- A system of communication that gets real-time information to the right people who can best use it.
- A system of reporting relationships and performance measurements that promote the stated goals of the organization.
- A system of internal benchmarking that learns from other areas of the company.
- Other systems particular to the industry or specialty of the organization.

All systems are designed to work with each other; there may be overlap by design. To be effective, accountability programs must draw from the systems and reinforce communication within the organization. The systems emphasize measurement and review. The leaders must set out to lead the building of these systems and implement them in an effective way.

My Experience

For years, I coached an otherwise brilliant client who saw opportunities around every corner and had a tendency to go after all of them, forgetting his accountability to the ongoing business and the stakeholders in it. The effect was detrimental to his business because he would constantly take his focus away from the ongoing business to attempt to pursue those shiny opportunities. It took my holding him accountable to get him to refocus on the business at hand and follow the strategic plan we had developed.

Another former client was an inventor who kept changing his focus and the focus of his business, according to his latest invention. The result was a business being run as a hobby shop and not the excellent manufacturing company it was supposed to be. He was not being accountable to the business and its people. The good news was that we both realized that his happiness was in the inventing part, and thus we changed the strategy of the business, making it a specialized shop. We developed a set of expectations, and together with his employees, we held him accountable to the new business strategy. The business thrived under this new direction, and the owner was very happy.

Employees and leaders who hold themselves accountable are a great benefit to their businesses. They are conscious of their impact on the bigger business picture and how their performance affects it. While admitting failures, they see them as opportunities to learn and to make corrections to prevent those failures from happening again. When leaders are willing to be held accountable, subordinates gain respect for them and, in turn, learn to hold themselves accountable, creating an enviable business environment. Senior leaders must openly promote, support, and reward accountability and lead by example. Without this culture, businesses will struggle to remain competitive.

As stated elsewhere in this book, a primary duty of management is hiring employees of all levels; the higher the level, the more critical the hire. The most important consideration when selecting employees is their fitness to the culture of the company, even more important than the candidate's qualifications for the job. Another key consideration is the candidate's ability to be accountable in the job. The hiring manager must have previously identified and documented the key accountabilities for the position. These accountabilities should be discussed with the candidate, and if a position of employment is reached, they should become part of the employment agreement.

Accountability and Delegation

Delegating is appointing someone else to act on one's behalf, meaning a managers or supervisors assign the authority and responsibility to another person to carry out certain tasks or activities they usually perform. Effective delegation is one of the most powerful activities in management because it enables managers to direct their focus and energy on those activities that only they can do. Delegation requires trust in the people assigned to do the job, and trust is the highest form of human motivation. By delegating, management is investing not only in the growth and development of the employee to whom the job is delegated, but also in the organization and in the manager. The ability to delegate will make this possible.

Delegation (appendix C) is the second-most difficult thing for managers to learn; delegating with accountability is *the* most difficult thing they can master. When one delegates, one is assigning the responsibility to answer for results; in other words, one is assigning accountability. Delegating without accountability is only distributing work. When accountability is not embraced, organizations can expect the prevalence of blame, unclear expectations, and even high turnover. Generally speaking, people want to see others held accountable and everyone treated the same and measured with the same yardstick. Without accountability, setting objectives is an exercise in futility.

Sadly, a majority of managers don't have a clue about how to hold people accountable, nor do they know how to hold themselves accountable. Many think they do, but in reality, they don't practice it effectively. Why is this? Why do most leaders have difficulty exercising proper accountability?

- They are used to working in a culture of conflict avoidance. It is much easier to let things go than to try to hold people accountable and face conflicts.
- They lack the skills to deal in accountability. It is a difficult thing to learn, and few people have the skills needed.

Typically, business executives are clearly inadequate in effectively setting expectations and holding others accountable for the results they are required to achieve. Consequently, accountability training is needed, not just for subordinates but also—and more importantly—for those at all management levels. Such training must be designed with a clear focus on the business results that the organization wants to achieve. Ensuring that those efforts are based on accountability will improve the chances for success. Moreover, implementing a positive approach to accountability will ensure that employees at all levels embrace individual accountable behavior.

Training for accountability must start with training in delegation and, therefore, as a component of delegation, in empowerment. To implement accountability in an organization, the leaders and supervisors must be able to delegate correctly and start by admitting that by delegating without holding people accountable, they are only distributing work. There are several concepts that must be taken into account when delegating:

- The first and perhaps most critical is to match the job to the people assigned to it. Does the people have the talent, training, expertise, and willingness to do the job? Are they truly available to do the job, or do they already have too many things on their plate?
- Delegating means giving up control. Is the manager willing to give it up? Is the employee able to receive it? Is the manager capable of empowering the employee, and is the employee capable of self-empowerment? The manager is still responsible for the job being delegated; is that understood?

- Obtain commitment from the employee to act with the added authority and corresponding responsibility. Employees must understand that with added responsibility also comes added accountability. They also need to clearly understand the possible rewards if they succeed and penalties if they fail.
- Provide the tools, facilities, and assistance that employees will need to successfully complete the job. Part of the assistance is to monitor the progress of the job (without micromanaging or interfering in the employee's work).
- Incentivize the employee by making clear the conditions for the work, what constitutes success, and how it will be rewarded. Most importantly, let the employees know they have the manager's full support and are a key part of the company's objectives.
- After the work is completed, review it to ensure it has met the expected results; if there are flaws or it misses the target, explain it in detail, provide help to correct the errors, and offer training to make sure it doesn't happen again. Be careful here, as the criticism provided must be constructive and not damaging to the employee's motivation.

Many employee incentives fail to motivate enough of the desired behavior; they end up becoming a permanent expense that only yields a temporary benefit. Management should choose methods of creating and maintaining incentives that avoid becoming entitlements and are positive enough to yield the desired results. Incentive plans, if not implemented correctly, can result in counterproductive behaviors, including resentment of employees. Especially in the area of sales, incentive plans should drive positive behaviors with positive results, rewarding the true accomplishments in a fair way and with equality.

A challenge for management is to identify what motivates different employees, since this varies. Money is always a motivator, but it's not always strong enough to motivate certain employees. Job advancement, title adjustment, public recognition, and praise can all be strong motivators. It is also important to offer rewards in a timely manner; this could be at the completion of a project or at specific steps in the process, but don't wait until the next salary review to give it. A motivated employee will make delegation much easier and effective.

Empowerment

Empowerment is a key component of delegation; without empowerment, delegation is just distributing work.

Without empowerment, there is no commitment; without commitment, there is no responsibility; and without responsibility, there is no accountability.

The definition of *empowerment* is to give power or authority; to authorize, especially by legal or official means. To give or delegate power or authority.

In business terms, empowerment is the process of enabling or authorizing an individual to think, behave, take action, and make decisions in autonomous ways. It is the state of feeling self-empowered to take control of one's destiny. As a broad definition, empowerment means giving employees the power to do their job.

Not empowering employees can significantly increase the cost of doing business. Create a more effective organization by giving your employees the information and authority to act and make decisions on their own, within a structured set of organizational goals and values. When you create a culture of empowerment, employees are free to use the knowledge they acquired, the experience they've gained, and the motivation of being a true part of the business. Empowered employees feel a sense of ownership in their projects, with the resulting excitement and motivation to perform. As owners of their projects, they become accountable for results, doubling the benefits to the organization.

Some managers view empowerment as giving people the power to make decisions, and some employees view empowerment as being given the freedom to do what they want to do, without regard for position or authority. In reality, it is a process to release the knowledge, experience, and motivation that is already in people but is being severely underutilized. Employees gain through empowerment a happier work environment and a sense of personal growth; companies gain a more efficient organization and a chance for continuous improvement through employee involvement.

The Three Keys to Empowerment

In their book, *The 3 Keys to Empowerment*, Ken Blanchard, John Carlos, and Alan Randolph propose a three-part process to create empowerment. These are the three keys:

- Share information with everyone. It's your responsibility as leader to share all information about the business (within limits, of course; not all information can be shared). Unless they have the information, employees will take empowerment as just another dictate from management. By having the information, they will feel that management is making them part of the business and will develop trust in management.
- Create autonomy through boundaries. This relates to the need for autonomy by establishing boundaries within which employees can determine what to do and how to do it. The boundaries are set by the leader, who declares certain areas off-limits, such as the company's vision and general management rules.
- Let teams become hierarchical. This calls for replacing the traditional hierarchy with self-directed teams. Empowered, self-directed teams are quite different from semiautonomous teams. They play a much more active role; they make decisions and are accountable for results. These teams require members to learn to function within their different charter.

If you are implementing a culture of empowerment, you will face some challenges. As with any cultural change and behavior adjustment of both leaders and employees, the process will involve many ups and downs along the way. To create a culture of empowerment, people must behave in different ways than would commonly occur in a hierarchical culture. This change of behavior involves a movement from dependence on the leadership of others to independence from, or interdependence with, external leadership, and these changes are not easy.

Empowerment can be difficult to achieve because of the requirement to create the culture. You can't tell employees to act empowered and expect them to do it; they need to be trained and coached on how to make decisions and in accepting responsibility for them.

The Benefits of Empowerment

There is no question as to the value of empowerment. Managers want employees who accept responsibility, have a proprietary interest in the company, and want to work hard to achieve good results. Employees, on the other hand, want to feel valued, be involved in their jobs, and be proud of the work they do. Essentially, then, managers and employees want the same thing, even if they do not realize it at first view. Employee satisfaction and the corresponding lower turnover, improved teamwork, improved customer service, and customer retention are perhaps more important benefits.

Workplace Empowerment

By empowering employees, you are providing them with opportunities and the freedom to make their own decisions with regards to their job. But providing freedom doesn't mean leaving them alone. For empowerment to work well, you need to be involved ... but not too involved. If you are not involved at all, you are not communicating, measuring, or coaching those you are empowering; you are sending the message that they are on their own, giving employees a sense of insecurity. This is just the opposite of what you want. If an employee or team fails, you are to blame for not providing them guidance. Conversely, if you are too involved, you are not demonstrating confidence in your employees. You undermine their authority by meddling in their work, and they become frustrated by your lack of trust. There is a delicate balance between the two situations, and you need to be sure of how to act based on the personalities involved, the training they have, and the complexity of their job.

There is a belief among business owners and leaders that some employees don't care and always try to do as little for the company as they can get away with. Such owners cannot implement empowerment until they first get over this thinking. The truth is that each case is unique; there is a wide spectrum of situations and of people, and you need to know your employees, yourself, and the work environment well enough to know where on the spectrum it is appropriate to start the process.

To create empowerment, the management role must change from a mind-set of being in control to an attitude of assigning responsibility and providing the supporting environment for employees to excel in their functions. People already have power in their knowledge and motivation; empowerment releases and focuses this power.

The key is for managers to understand that empowerment involves releasing the power people already have and for employees to realize that empowerment also means greater responsibilities, accountability, and opportunities to advance. If both parts adopt these concepts, both will benefit, and together, they will benefit the company. The leader is responsible for teaching the concept to the staff and creating a culture to make it "the way we work here."

Leadership has the responsibility to create the work environment that will foster the ability and desire of employees to act in empowered ways, and to remove barriers that limit this ability. Unless empowerment starts at the top, it's going nowhere; it's up to the leader to make it successful.

Benefits of self-managed teams:

- increased job satisfaction
- attitude change from "have to" to "want to"
- greater employee commitment
- better communication between employees and management
- more efficient decision-making process
- improved quality
- reduced operating costs
- more profitable organization

The Process of Empowerment

Empowerment is a process that includes the following components:

- You're confident that the employee has the capabilities and resources needed to do the job.
- You set clear expectations regarding the job and expected outcomes.
- You communicate work goals and department processes, and share all information you have regarding problems or challenges.
- You show your commitment and support to employees by guiding them without interfering.
- You establish metrics in advance and make it clear what the department and company standards are.
- You hold employees accountable; they are accountable for the solution and learn from any problems or mistakes committed. How much support you give them will depend on their level, their knowledge, and the complexity of the job.
- In order to get the most out of your staff, you need to learn how to empower employees effectively and allow them to use their unique skills to solve problems.
- You listen to employees. Because they work at their jobs every day, they can contribute with viable suggestions for ways to increase efficiency.

- You're willing to allow employees to fail; this sends the message that you have given them the power and are not going to second-guess them. A second benefit is that they will learn from their mistakes.
- Remember that empowering employees does not mean giving up all control. You are still in charge, and you are still responsible for the final outcome. As such, you need to retain some control and measure progress.

Empowered employees add value to the company, so by learning how to empower employees, you are helping your strong business grow even stronger. Using the talents that are already on your payroll is one way to build a competitive advantage in your market.

The Credo of an Empowering Manager

You want to create an environment for people to feel empowered, productive, contributing, and happy. Don't handicap them by limiting the tools they need. Trust them to do the right thing and get out of their way. (Trust but verify). These are the most important principles for empowering people in a way that reinforces accomplishment, and contribution.

- Demonstrate that you value people. Help people feel that they are part of something bigger than themselves and their individual job. Do this by making sure they know and have access to the organization's overall mission, vision, and strategic plans.
- Share goals and direction. Empowered employees can then chart their course without constant supervision. Trust the intentions of people to do the right thing, make the right decision, and make choices that, while maybe not exactly what you would decide, still work. When employees receive clear expectations from you, they relax and trust you.

- Delegate authority and impact opportunities, not just more work. Do not just delegate the drudge work; delegate some of the fun stuff too.
- Provide frequent feedback so that people know how they are doing. Sometimes, the purpose of feedback is reward and recognition as well as improvement coaching.
- Solve problems, don't pinpoint problem people. When a problem occurs, ask what is wrong with the work system that caused the people to fail, not what is wrong with the people.
- Listen to learn and ask questions to provide guidance. Guide by asking questions, not by telling grown-ups what to do.

The Ladder of Accountability

InfoPro Learning developed a tool to determine the level of accountability in an organization and assess where people are located on this spectrum, visualized as a ladder. This was reported by Rodger Dean Duncan, explaining that the ladder consists of eight rungs and a base; it's divided in two sections of four rungs. The base is defined as people being unaware or unconscious; they don't even know there is a situation that needs attention. As we go up the ladder, the next rung is categorized as "Blame Others." This is where the finger-pointing prevails, and the faults are always someone else's. One step above this one is the "Personal Excuses" level where people, as the name indicates, find all kinds of excuses to justify their failure.

The next rung up the ladder is the "I Can't" level, where people claim they are unable to perform what's wanted of them; it isn't their fault because they are controlled by circumstances. The next level is "Wait and Hope," where people place the obligation for results on others. All these actions described on the lower half of the ladder are considered victim behaviors; people on these rungs believe that things happen to them because of circumstances beyond their control.

As we move to the upper half of the ladder, the next rung is "Acknowledge Reality," in which people see the situation for what it is and realize that something needs to be done to change the status, but they are not the ones to do it. The next step is "Embrace It," and people classified as such admit their own role in the problem and accept ownership of the situation. Since they own the problem, they are more willing to solve it than those who only recognize that the problem exists. The next step up is "Find a Solution," representing those who strive to solve the problem and work to find an answer.

The last step and highest on the ladder is "Make It Happen," representing people who not only recognize and accept the problem and work to find a solution, but they also get results. The upper half of the ladder represents accountable behaviors, describing those who make things happen; good things happen because of them.

People on the highest rung often make others uncomfortable because they cannot accept half-done solutions and gain satisfaction from solving even the most difficult situations or problems that others can't—or won't—solve. They enjoy knowing that things happen because of them, not *to* them. They feel accountable for results and accountable to other members of the team, and of course, this includes accepting responsibility when personal performance fails. They also enjoy credit for personal performance excellence.

The Culture of Accountability

There is a popular phrase that says, "If you can't define your culture, then the culture defines you." Every organization must have a system that defines how the business operates, identifies measures to prevent or correct unexpected events, ad describes ongoing operational rules. Without such a system, situational happenings will drive the culture. The culture must foster empathy in the workplace and create an engaged workforce to maximize productivity; it should be such that employees know that management cares for them. The system must create a culture that brings meaning into the employee's professional life and builds a sense of purpose to all. Dale Carnegie said, "Inaction breeds doubt and fear; action breeds confidence and courage." Take action, and define the culture of the organization.

Company-wide accountability is a key element to making a business sustainable over the long term. Organizations that master this value consistently have higher levels of employee morale and significantly outperform companies that do not embrace it. Building accountability at all levels of the company is key to making a business sustainable. What makes accountability so critical is that without it, you and your organization will suffer. Without accountability throughout the organization, the result is chaos.

Accountability is a company's way of life. It is how a business functions, how the employees behave, how management acts, and how the company interacts with the outside world. The owners or entrepreneurs who start the venture, the leaders, establish what culture they want to reign in the company and do what's necessary to implement it. The culture must be based on the leaders' core values and reflect how they want those values to form the DNA of the company. Leaders are also governed by the culture created and must lead by example by adhering to the rules of the culture. Those rules are transmitted to the management team and downwards to each employee. Accountability must be one of the key fundamentals of the culture, and as such, it must be adhered to by all, from the beginning.

As with any piece of company culture, it is much easier to create and implement a culture of accountability in a young organization as opposed to a long-established one. As a business grows and more employees become part of it, it's essential for leaders to establish accountability for all tasks. As explained earlier, accountability starts with clarity in job descriptions and the instructions to carry on specific tasks. Goals and targets must be clearly communicated—preferably in writing—and acknowledged by the recipient of the instructions. Goals should be developed for the completion of a project and for specific stages, based on defined milestones at each step on the way to completion of a job. They should be visited at each step rather than waiting for the completion, when it may be too late to correct any deficiencies encountered along the way.

When two companies merge, the success of the new company resides in the compatibility of the two cultures being merged. Successful mergers are not guaranteed, regardless of the successful financial performance of both companies, and the failure of the marriage is often dependent on how accountable each company is; in other words, do the two cultures emphasize accountability the same way? I have seen mergers of two apparently successful companies fail for this reason. If one of the companies has a loose way of managing, while the other has a marked accountability culture, chances of a successful merger are low. Employees of the loose company will have a hard time adapting to the rules of their new partners, and at the very least, they will see those rules as dictatorial and penalizing. Changing the culture of this company would be a cumbersome and difficult project.

My Experience

I have had the fortunate (sometimes unfortunate) experience of working with many family businesses. One of them involved three brothers who were appointed co-owners by the exiting father. They were also given equal levels of responsibilities, with authority over three separate areas of the business. The brothers did not take this split well, resulting in much resentment and infighting. Their relationship was so bad that they hardly spoke to each other, acting as leaders of three separate companies and showing a lack of accountability to the entire company. Unfortunately, the business showed the bad karma and was floundering.

Reacting to our encouragement, all three joined separate peer boards that a colleague and I chaired. We got them involved in a strategic planning process and in intensive personal accountability training as a way to get them to talk with each other, and we had coaching sessions individually with each of them and as a group. Gradually, the relationships improved significantly, and it was reflected in the success of the business and in their happiness as individuals and as a family. Had the succession taken a different approach, emphasizing teamwork and team accountability, the differences could have been avoided.

Chapter 3 Takeaways

Change only happens when individuals are motivated from within.
- All employees, not just management, have to step up and be more accountable, not only for their personal results but for the organization's results.
- Adding accountability to the typical organization chart provides clarity about who occupies the primary roles and responsibilities for which they are accountable.
- When leaders are willing to accept being accountable, subordinates gain respect for them and in turn learn to hold themselves accountable.
- Delegation with accountability is the most difficult thing for a manager to master.
- Training for accountability must start with training in delegation and in empowerment.
- By empowering employees, you are providing them with the freedom to make their own decisions with regards to their job.
- Empowerment involves releasing the power people already have.
- Company-wide accountability is a key element to making a business sustainable over the long term.

CHAPTER FOUR
PERSONAL ACCOUNTABILITY

Cultural Value

Truly, there is one core cultural value that no truly successful organization can do without: personal accountability. Personal accountability requires team members to take responsibility for their own actions and help other members take responsibility. They also improve the performance of the organization by focusing on actions to take at the individual level.

Personal accountability focuses on the outcomes that are at the end of process. In reality, personal accountability encompasses all phases of the process: before, during, and after. Throughout the process of personal accountability, one must be willing to personally take ownership for

- understanding and accepting the task,
- taking actions to achieve agreed-upon results, and
- answering the results obtained, regardless of the outcome.

Accountability is related to give an account of

- what you accepted as your responsibility,
- what resources were assigned to you,

- what you accomplished with them, and
- what results you produced.

It is advisable to form a team to help individuals develop a plan and execute specific tasks needed to accomplish in each of the areas. Develop goals set for a period, discuss anticipated issues, and set SMART (Specific, Measurable, Achievable, Relevant, and Time-Bound) goals for the period.

In the "Culture of Accountability" section, we said that every organization has a set of unique values that define its culture; in most cases, the organization's culture is a reflection of the personal values of its founder and how the founder or its leader implemented those values throughout the organization. In my experience, coaching dozens of leaders of small and midsize businesses and executives in all types of industries, there is one cultural value that is key to the success of any organization, and that is personal accountability. It is really a cultural value that requires all team members to assume responsibility for their own and each other's actions and to focus on the actions required at the individual and team level to improve individual performance and, therefore, increase the performance of the organization.

The organization's core values determine its identity, and I judge personal accountability as a principal component of that identity. Personal accountability requires having the courage to accept responsibility; by definition, you are causing something to happen, and by being accountable, you are responsible for your behavior. Accountability also means admitting mistakes and committing to meeting agreed-upon expectations. Accountable people accept the consequences of the choices they make; they do what's right just because it's the right thing to do.

Personal accountability is not a trait that people are born with; it is a way of living and acting that they can learn. It starts by defining your role and determining what you are responsible for; you cannot be personally accountable unless you're clear on what your responsibilities are. You must admit your weaknesses and have the self determination to change weaknesses into strengths. You must be honest in accepting your errors and be resolute to fix them and learn to prevent them. You must be aware of how you use your time and learn to manage it carefully so you don't take on more than you can handle.

Lack of personal accountability may indicate that someone is more concerned with outward appearance and image than with results and success. People with this trait will seek to blame others or outside factors rather than admit fault; they believe that protecting their self-image is more important than correcting the problems. To be personally accountable, one must look in a mirror and ask, "What am I doing wrong (or not doing right), and what can I do to solve the problem?" An honest self-analysis of our actions should tell us if we are acting with the right attitude toward responsibility and accountability; we must be honest in our self-perception.

Organizations that stress personal accountability as a core value have higher levels of employee morale and outperform organizations that do not. These five signs indicate that personal accountability is not a core value:

1. When everything is everyone else's fault and complaints between department are frequent. Excuses multiply and finger-pointing at everyone other than at oneself is prevalent.
2. When people complain about new concepts and use this as an excuse for failing to reach business objective and not living up to expectations.
3. When people feel they are not being appreciated and voice their frustration by allowing opportunities to slip by and pushing deadlines past their original date.
4. When people complain about not having support and blame a lack of resources available to them.
5. When people feel it's just a job and are not attuned to the organization's mission and values; performance suffers as a result.

Values are essential to the organization's identity and the most critical value to its success is personal accountability. It can be integrated into the organization's culture regardless of what other values it has. The best thing about personal accountability is that it is a value that can be consciously adapted as a core cultural value. If any of the five items above describe your organization there is a good chance that it lacks personal accountability as a core cultural value

Larry and Michael Cole and Byrd Baggett tell us that "your perception of me is more important than my perception of me." This means that you may believe you are an excellent performer, but it is important to portray an image of accountability to be more respected by the team and be recognized as an accountable person. So it follows that you should ensure that the coworkers have the same perception that you have of yourself. Cole, Cole, and Baggett also tell us that every action has a consequence, and we have much to gain by exhibiting accountability. They list the following advantages of being accountable:

- You are trusted.
- You are respected.
- You send the message that you are willing to do whatever is necessary for the success of the team.
- You are a high-performing professional.
- Your job security is likely increased.
- You improve the likelihood of being promoted.
- You can be trusted to complete challenging and meaningful assignments.

Of course, the consequences of not being accountable are the opposite of the advantages listed.

You set goals—personal, work, society—and do everything you need to do and learn everything you need to achieve those goals, but are you motivated? Do you have the personal commitment to do it? For example, I've wanted to write this book for a long time, but I didn't think I had the motivation and patience to do it. I used all typical excuses, such as "I don't have the time," or "I'm already involved in other projects," or "My consulting takes priority," or "My CEO clients want me to spend more time with them," and thus, the book didn't get written. But then, I decided I had to do it. I set a starting date and decided on some simple targets to accomplish. I used my self-empowerment, put aside other tasks, and gave this book the priority it needed to be done.

Now I had to hold myself accountable for the commitment I made, and so I started with a plan. I chose a starting date, immediately following the completion of an important project I had. I cleared my to-do list for that day and a couple of days after. I marked a calendar with that date and specified a couple of other days, about a week apart, to check on the progress of my commitment, and I placed the calendar in a very visible place. I chose this mundane way of tracking because it is easy to do, it is more visible, and I get the satisfaction of crossing out the accomplished dates. As I reached each intermediate goal, I set new goals and continued with this process. There were steps where I needed the contribution of other people to accomplish, but I set goals for that too and tried (when possible) to hold those people accountable. I am proud to say that I met most of my goals and that—as you can see by reading it—I accomplished the main goal of writing the book.

My Experience

A client of mine suffered from optimisms, an illness that affects the thought process of smart and cautious business owners. He had the ability to see opportunities much before they were apparent and was convinced that they were coming his way. He had a habit of building his organization to a level he thought the opportunity would demand, obviously forgetting his personal responsibility to accomplish the strategic plan of the company.

Unfortunately, those opportunities didn't always materialize, and he had to release the extra personnel not needed for the actual level of business. This fault in personal accountability clearly had an impact on his finances, but the most damaging impact was in the morale of the organization; people heard great promises of growth that never materialized, and they saw workers getting let go because of the CEO's unrealistic planning.

I had the opportunity to work with another owner who had the opposite disease: exaggerated conservatism. This condition prevented him from hiring people ahead of the needs of increased demand for the business. As a result, he often got into a panic mode of hiring because the performance of the business was suffering. Hiring in a panic invariably results in mistakes (hiring the wrong people), and the organization as a whole suffers. Thus, his operating mode had a double negative effect of poor performance (late deliveries, poor quality) and loss of opportunities (not being ready for them).

These examples show that you need to be personally accountable to the needs of the business. Being aware of opportunities is great, but use caution and be personally accountable to the needs of the organization.

So my advice to hold yourself accountable for your own projects is to first, clarify in your mind what you want to accomplish, and make sure it is within your capabilities. Then set a plan detailing the dates, efforts, partial goals, contributions needed from others, and everything you can think of to help you achieve your main goal. Make this plan as simple as possible, as you don't want to be overwhelmed with unnecessary details and create motivational steps along the way to continuously fan the flame of accountability. It can also help to make other people aware of what you are doing—your spouse, a colleague, or a friend. This obligates you to do what you say you'd do, if nothing else out of discomfort for letting others know that you failed. At each step, review your progress, make yourself accountable for any failings or triumphs, and take the necessary corrections.

To assume self-accountability for tasks or projects within an organization, use a similar approach, adjusting it for the conditions of the job and team environment. If you are a member of a team, assume responsibility for your job, and hold yourself accountable for your accomplishment (or lack thereof). Accountability is a personal trait that spans both private and professional lives. It is what makes individuals do what it takes to achieve the goals and desired outcomes while complying with a company's (or society's) policies. It requires the willingness and ability to assume ownership for individual actions and their consequences.

My Experience

One CEO I was coaching had a problem with a vice president of his company. He was a very capable executive with excellent technical aptitude but an accountability issue; he wanted to be liked by all and was more preoccupied with solving individual problems of others than with his performance toward the functioning of the company. Whenever someone asked him for help fixing something or solving a personal problem, he would work readily and efficiently on that but forget his own areas of responsibility, therefore allowing his work to suffer. I coached him to set up short-term goals related to his responsibility, and I held him accountable for meeting (or not meeting) those goals. It was hard for him to say no to requests from others, who were used to him responding to those requests, but after a while, and after he was able to see the difference in his performance and the recognition from the CEO, he became self-motivated and an excellent contributor to the goals of the company.

Personal accountability is a critical step toward improving leadership. When people are accountable for their own decisions, work, and results, the organization becomes more effective. A leader must give to employees as much control as possible to see accountability increase exponentially. Individualism in being responsible for the work one does is a great motivator that drives accountability. Joseph Folkman reported the results of the assessments done on forty thousand leaders who scored very high on effectiveness for accountability and found eight traits linked to high personal accountability:

1. Honesty and integrity. Accountable people do not hide negative information; if a project is behind schedule, they readily admit it without using excuses. When managers and leaders are open and direct, employees are more willing to be open too.
2. Drive for results. Clearly define the results that you want your people to deliver, and then give them control over how they deliver those results (obviously, they must follow certain guidelines tied to the overall goals of the company and the rules of the organization).
3. Trust. The three pillars that build trust and accountability are a leader's positive relationships, knowledge, and consistency. The research shows that people don't trust leaders when they are not confident that their efforts will be rewarded, when they suspect that leadership may take advantage of them and not credit them for their accomplishments, and when they don't trust the leader's motives.
4. Clear vision and direction. People cannot be accountable if they are not absolutely clear about the organization's vision, direction, and goals.
5. Problem solving and technical expertise. To ensure that people are accountable, teach them the skills they need and give them the support they require so they feel confident in doing their job.
6. Communication. A critical part of the process of accountability is two-way communication. Leaders and subordinates must be willing and able to openly and clearly communicate.
7. Ability to change. Organizations that are good at accepting and creating change have employees who operate at a high level of accountability. Both leaders and employees are effective at accepting feedback, taking on challenges, innovating, spreading optimism, showing concern, and seeing clear goals.

8. Collaborating and resolving conflict. Teams that cooperate are far more successful than those that compete. Cooperation breeds accountability, and great accountability in the organization begins with you and each member.

Kathy Koehler gives us six steps for increasing accountability:

1. Identify your picture of success and desired outcome for the most important things such as yourself, family, friends, performance at work, community, and spiritual growth.
2. Develop a few nonnegotiable commitments you are willing to make to achieve your desired outcome.
3. Create a recovery plan when you find yourself breaking those commitments.
4. Assess any commitments that others ask you to make in order to stay consistent with what you define as success, and have the courage to say no if a new commitment interferes with your nonnegotiable commitments.
5. If you cannot support other people, try to help them to find a new solution so they can achieve their success.
6. Acknowledge yourself for every commitment you keep that reinforces your picture of success, but also acknowledge commitments that you break that will prevent you from acting consistent with your values.

Self-Empowerment

"That's not my job." "I couldn't get the information." "I didn't have time to finish." "I didn't have the authority to do it." "I couldn't get the help that I needed." These excuses have negative effects on any organization's performance and quality of service. But how do you prevent this from affecting your organization? By creating a culture that encourages (or in some cases even demands) ownership of tasks; in other words, empowering people to assume full responsibility for the tasks they are to do. And the best practice to achieve this is self-empowerment.

Empowerment is a management style that enables employees to use their skills and abilities to benefit themselves and, as a result, benefit the organization as well. Employees working in a culture that promotes empowerment feel a sense of ownership in their projects that motivates them to perform to the best of their abilities. As owners, they are responsible for their projects and become accountable for results, doubling the benefits to the organization. Employees feel encouraged to use the knowledge and experience they acquired by that freedom and are motivated to be a true part of the business. The organization has the responsibility to create a work environment that helps foster the desire of employees to act in empowered ways. It is also responsible for removing any barriers that keep employees from acting in empowered ways.

The Value of a Personal Accountability Plan

Many benefits can be expected from having a personal accountability plan:

- Reduced worry. Personal accountability allows you to start and complete actions that need to be done.
- Reliance on others. Working with others to hold them accountable allows you to better see options and determine how you can harness the strengths of others; it also brings some objectivity to the situation.
- Focus on what is important by prioritizing tasks.
- Higher levels of attentiveness. Focus on clients and coworkers and give them the attention they need.

The downside of personal accountability is that it is tough to do. Having to explain your actions may be humbling, and taking directions from others may also be difficult. Of course, there are also downsides when personal accountability is lacking; most likely, they will be more critical. Without personal accountability

- there will be more stress,
- it robs productivity,
- it typically results in wasted time,
- it makes the job less attractive, and
- it may affect relationships.

Considering the benefits of personal accountability, it's surprising it isn't practiced more often in the business environment.

Your Personal Accountability System

A difficult challenge in achieving goals is simply focusing on them and staying on track. We are continuously interrupted by external influences that distract us from the goals: phone calls, emails, postal mail, urgent memos, unexpected visitors, and new items to add to the to-do list. New things can take our minds away from important things. We must therefore force ourselves back to the goals, reviewing them and prioritizing them again if necessary. We must not be lured into working on what we like or what's urgent but not important. It's a process of constantly rechecking the list and figuring out the correct next step.

We are tempted to work on what we like or what is easier or what yields an immediate sense of accomplishment. But the primary goals are not automatic, and each one may require much effort. So how do we to stay focused on the primary goals, despite the pressure to work on other things? It helps to maintain a personal accountability system. This can simply be a three-ring binder that contains the goals by period, the complete list of projects or tasks, and the actions list.

Keep this binder within sight and visit it often, usually many times per day. Read the goals frequently, note which are the most important, and label them as such. It's a process of constantly rechecking that we are still on course and making adjustments as needed. Break projects and actions into two parts: primary and secondary. The primary projects and next actions lead directly to the primary goals. The secondary projects and next actions lead to secondary goals (they may not even be linked to the goals). I suggest spending at least 50 percent of each day working on the primary goals; go straight to the next actions list and start working on the primary actions.

By monitoring our progress, we can see many actions we've completed from the primary list or whether we slipped to the secondary list. This is one way of keeping score; check it every day and always know our focus. The system promotes accountability, and by using it every day, we can view the project it links to and see the goal behind it. By focusing on a few primary goals, each in a different area of life, it's always clear which goal we should be working on. This prevents us from deviating off course.

The personal accountability system is just one tool for staying on track. Accountability exists at all levels and is an integral part of life. Without continuously focusing on the important goals, it's just too easy to get sidetracked. The system provides an answer to the question, how do we accomplish this? How do we do what is needed to contribute to our own success or to the success of our team? Implementing the system will also move us toward personal accountability, for us and our team members.

Accountability—like most things—starts at the top. You have to hold yourself accountable and set an example before you can expect to hold others accountable. This is a measure of your capacity to be answerable for your personal actions. Personal accountability is leadership by example. Leaders who have mastered personal accountability will inspire their subordinates to exhibit the same behaviors and encourage leadership development within the team. Accountability is not something you make people do; you must implement the culture and have people accept and buy into the concept. You need to understand that this may be a new, unfamiliar way to work for your employees, and therefore, you need to teach and coach the concept as a benefit and not as a penalty.

My Experience

This is another example of the lack of personal accountability at the top. I'm an admirer of Jack Welch and his teachings from the experience he gained as CEO of one of the largest companies of the country. However, he's not a shining example of personal accountability. Case in point: In *Winning*, while writing about hiring and selecting the right people, he admits to having picked the right people only 50 percent of the time as a young manager, later improving to 80 percent. While this batting average may be good for his management philosophy, it is a disaster for those suffering the penalty of his lack of accountability in selecting the right people.

Furthermore, he preaches, "Don't beat yourself up if you are hiring wrong some of the time." I beg to differ with him on this too. Hiring wrong is not only a killer for a small business, it's also a killer in people selection and management. He should have adopted self-accountability to make people selection a high priority talent to be developed. When you make a hiring mistake, you must not only correct it as soon as it is detected as a mistake, but you must learn your lesson, decide where you went wrong, and take the necessary measures to prevent the mistake from happening again.

Personal accountability is essential for any successful organization. When employees take ownership of their projects and accept responsibility for results, the entire company benefits. To foster a culture of accountability, leaders must model specific behaviors of each employee, considering their personalities and adaptability to new concepts.

Personal accountability is natural in some people who have an inclination toward it, but it can also be learned. Teach employees to be personally accountable, and they will understand that they can affect their situations. They are not victims of external factors but authors of their own lives. With this knowledge, they will feel capable of handling any challenge and enjoy real happiness, both personally and professionally. To help your team achieve a greater sense of accountability, stop trying to make them feel immune to pain and guilt; equip them instead with what they need to face the challenges present at work. The following are suggestions to develop accountability in employees:

- Hold them accountable on a consistent basis, by people and processes, to get them used to the mind-set of internal accountability. Eventually, they will accept that their results are a product of their own actions.
- Provide consistent, regular, and rigorous feedback to help employees understand how their specific behaviors contribute to the results they get.
- Teach employees to engage in self-analysis about their progress, accounting for their role in the results obtained and developing the lessons that will empower them to a better result.

With this training, they will be able to adopt a different, more sustainable approach to their engagement in their work. This will help create a workforce that is resilient, is committed to results, and accepts the consequences of their actions, whether they are good or bad. By implementing this culture, they will make great things happen for the business and develop their own sense of responsibility as well. When you hold team members accountable, it's a way of expressing that you value them and their place on the team.

Even after leaders equip teams with information and training, the teams need someone to push them to reach their potential, to rise to the standard, or simply to practice the behaviors that will lead to success. The process starts with celebrating personal accountability at every level within the organization.

Mary Barra, CEO of General Motors, is changing the culture that's been ingrained in the company for many years. She is changing what other CEOs haven't been able to fix. Changing the culture means changing behaviors. Culture is how people behave, and in GM, people try hard not to bring bad news to higher-ups; it's been that way for decades, but now, she is changing it. Practically no one is ever accountable for a decision because most decisions are made by committees; virtually no one was ever fired for performance. She takes a different approach to management; she says, "I'm not asking people to do something; I'm telling them to do it. It is a requirement to hold themselves accountable. It isn't optional throughout the organization."

She asked all executives the following: "If you could change one behavior, what would it be?" One of the answers she got was "driving accountability," owning each other's problems, a relentless desire to win but having candor and transparency. She listened and acted on it, and people started to behave that way.

Seven previous CEOs since the 1980s tried to change the culture, but the culture won. It remains to be seen if she is able to do it fully. Other companies have had similar cultures, and some strong leaders have been able to alter them. Welch did it in General Electric in the 1980s, Lou Gerstner did it at IBM in the 1990s, and Doug Conant did it at Campbell's Soup in the 2000s. However, the change failed at other well-known companies because changing a deep-rooted culture is not easy, particularly when accountability is the major issue.

In a company that has a culture of accountability, people do what they commit to do. Conversely, if an organization lacks accountability, there will be a tendency to live by a flood of excuses for not meeting objectives. If "good enough" is accepted as good, and "no one will notice the difference" is an acceptable mantra, or worse yet, if objectives are seen as arbitrary and stupid, the company can suffer the consequences of low morale, low quality, and higher costs.

With accountability comes a measure of discipline. Accountability is a synonym of responsibility and the opposite of permissiveness. Holding people accountable is really about discipline and the distribution of power. Individuals have more purpose when they accept accountability and have the power of responsibility. When people become more responsible, they can have more freedom. Creating an environment where accountability can take root and blossom isn't easy, but you don't have to make it harder than it is. You need to understand what motivates people to become more empowered, responsible, and accountable, without resorting to punitive measures. With this knowledge, you coach them to accept the fact that being accountable means to have more power over what they do, and the satisfaction of being their own overseer with respect to the completion of high-quality projects.

Accountability has very little to do with titles or positioning; it has everything to do with responsibility at all levels of the organization, not just managers or supervisors. Position-based, command-and-control management is completely obsolete when accountability is the culture. There are still reporting levels and varying degrees of responsibility, but in this culture, everyone is accountable for their projects, regardless of how the tasks are assigned. Within this culture, teamwork is fomented because the actions and results of each member affects the team, and thus, members are motivated to go the extra mile to help coworkers and also to drive colleagues to be accountable.

To build company-wide accountability, one must stop doing things that can undermine it. Things like overseeing, micromanaging, and looking over people's shoulder take away from employee self-motivation and individualism; they prevent accountability. Conversely, companies that can clearly articulate, promote, and execute their strategies and goals are well positioned to create accountability throughout the organization. One must start by deciding what's important, including the vision, mission, and strategic values. Develop the strategies based on the plan, and develop the goals to achieve the strategies. Align the systems to support the goals; execute the plan according to the activities assigned to each employee. Identify problems and their source, and develop actions to eliminate them and prevent them in the future. Lastly, develop leadership not just at the top but throughout the employee force. Building a culture of accountability requires an organization that is ready and able to accept it.

Am I proposing a hypothetical organization? Would this be impossible to achieve? Most definitely not. It is very achievable if you as the manager/leader put the emphasis in the culture, and you dedicate the effort to educate all your subordinates and peers (and yourself) in the requirements and benefits to be enjoyed. Building a strong culture within a team is at the core of business success. You want a culture that recognizes and embraces shared values, attitudes, standards, and beliefs that characterize the goals of the organization. And it's a good idea to make sure it suits the best people who work at the company while making a positive impression on customers and anyone else associated with the business. Establishing a culture you believe in means having a clear and consistent vision and knowing how you'd like everyone, inside and outside, to view the company. Many old-school CEOs and leaders were often "business operations first and people second," but it's the people who make a business successful.

My Experience

A CEO I was coaching complained of being constantly bothered with interruptions by colleagues asking him to make decisions that other people should have been able to make. My analysis of the situation indicated that he had created a culture of going to the top for almost everything that needed a decision. This culture was not created by design; it had grown from a nontolerance by the CEO of decisions made by others that he did not agree with.

It was clearly a combination of nonempowerment and a belief that he was the only one who could make the right decisions. It took some time and much coaching to change his attitude toward others' decisions and then for him to learn to empower employees to make those decisions. Without empowerment, there is no responsibility and, therefore, no accountability. After the changes, he became much happier and the organization much more effective and efficient.

In an organization with a culture of accountability, people assume responsibility for a project, task, or action. People commit to a result before they even take action. Success or failure is up to them; they are responsible for their actions, and once they assume responsibility, they are all in, regardless of how the project goes. If it goes well, it is time for them to accept credit for it and enjoy the triumph. If for whatever reason it fails (in results, in time, in schedule, or in whatever form), it is time for them to accept full responsibility and work on actions to make sure it doesn't happen again. Supervisors and managers must give people responsibilities, not just jobs.

A solid business culture that foments accountability includes the following:

1. Transparency. The goal is for all employees, regardless of position, to feel they belong as a key members of the organization, to know the thinking, responsibilities, and strategies at all levels of the company, and to share ideas and feedback, no matter who they are. This in turn calls for responsibility and, therefore, accountability.
2. Empowerment and a sense of freedom. Empower people by not micromanaging but keeping employees aware of what they need to know. Informed employees are more involved and empowered in a company. The more freedom people have to take on tasks and to manage and execute them, the more they feel connected to the company's culture.
3. Physical space. Open spaces are great for some, but other people need to be able to close the door to be at their most productive. It's important to consider the comfort level of employees before deciding how to lay out space or selecting what type of office space to lease.
4. Talking to customers and employees. At different points in a company's maturation process, there are almost always periods of uncertainty. If the leader is having challenges relating to the product or corporate vision, the natural tendency is to turn his attention to what went wrong; talking to customers may help.
5. Your organizational design. Organizational design is the process, structure, and hierarchy put into place that allows the team to put the culture into practice. It is the "how you do things" that governs the norms of the company. It includes

communication, company policies, team building, performance indicators, performance evaluations, division of responsibilities, and even how to schedule and run meetings.
6. Time to disconnect. We all need to hit the reset button once in a while; people can't work long hours constantly without getting burned out at some point. While owners want employees to have a founder's mentality regarding hard work, they need to recognize the work-life balance that must exist; this balance is important in people's productivity.

Promoting a balance between work and personal life is a big part of actually being able to be held accountable; if employees are burned out, overworked, unhappy about working conditions, or feel underpaid, they won't accept being held accountable. If employees feel they are being abused or unrecognized, they will not care about being accountable.

An organization's culture is ideally formed by the personal values of its founder/owner and affected either positively or negatively by personal behaviors of all members. Personal behaviors consequently influence the culture of accountability in the organization.

The Main Aspects of Human Behavior

These are the main aspects of human behavior:

1. Psychology: the science of human behavior; people's behavior refers to anything they do. Behaviors have three aspects:

    - Cognition: to become aware of or know something (i.e., the job or tasks the employee is responsible for and the requirements of the job)
    - Affection: to have a certain feeling about it; how performance will be judged
    - Conation: to act in a particular way or direction after the feeling; agreement or disagreement with it

Human behavior may be covert (expressed inside) or overt (expressed outside). Dissatisfaction of employees with judgment of their performance may be expressed verbally or in negative behavior in the job. Negative behavior will undoubtedly affect acceptance of responsibility and consequent accountability.

2. Personality: the unique, integrated, and organized system of all behavior of a person. A person's physical traits, attitudes, habits, and emotional/psychological characteristics are all parts of their personality. Personality types include introverted and extroverted. The introvert generally shuns social contacts and is inclined to be solitary, whereas the extrovert seeks social contacts and enjoys them. It follows that some people may express feelings by discussing them with supervisors or coworkers, while others may suffer in silence, affecting their performance at work. Responsibility and accountability will likely be affected.
3. Interest: a preference for one activity over another. An interest is shown when a person voluntarily participates in an activity. Accepting responsibility for tasks or projects and therefore being accountable for the results are psychological effects of interest.
4. Attitude: a state of readiness, organized through experience, exerting an influence upon the individual's response to all situations with which it is related. Attitudes have certain characteristics:

- They are formed in relation to objects, persons, and values and are a result of an individual's contact with the environment and its requirements. They can be exhibited as positive or negative, obviously affecting the performance of the individual.

- They are prone to change brought about by training and other instructional methods. A negative attitude toward accountability can be changed by training and improving the team work environment.

5. Emotions: a state of being moved, stirred up, or aroused and involve impulses, feelings, and physical/psychological reactions. A negative emotional response may lead to a lack of cooperation and participation in programs, a work stoppage, or even destruction of the work done, obviously impacting accountability.
6. Wishes: a pattern of behavior that involves anticipated future satisfaction people believe is reasonably likely and toward which they usually relate some of their present behavior. A wish to change rules, for example, may drive someone to a negative or positive condition affecting behavior and consequently performance.
7. Judgment: opinions formed before due examination and consideration of facts and based on certain assumptions. Prejudices may lead to a hostile attitude toward persons or objects. Creating a culture of accountability, if not done right, may lead to prejudgment and rejection of the rule.
8. Frustration: a condition in which an individual perceives a goal as being blocked or unattainable. This creates tension. When faced with such a situation, the individual tries to make several kinds of adjustments in the behavior pattern. Again, the wrong application of accountability in an organization will create tension among its members, who will try to adjust their behavior to cope with a new rule they view as unfair.
9. Projection: in order to escape from facing the reality that they have failed, people may blame others or even a nonexistent factor. This is typical when people lack personal accountability.

Balancing Work and Life

Your business should be a part of your life apart from your life; it should not be your life.

As an entrepreneur and the person in charge, you are in control of your time, and time is your most precious asset. Because you are in control, you can fall into the trap of allowing the demands of your work to come at the expense of your family or your health. We talk about time management, but we must realize that we can't manage time; we can only manage how we use it. And how we use it determines, to a large extent, how we balance our life and our business.

Life is inherently stressful, but identifying our principal values and goals allows us to concentrate on what is most important to us and decide what sacrifices we must make to achieve those goals. For most entrepreneurs, career becomes the focus by default, but in making that choice, they risk losing other valuable assets such as health or family. Balancing life and business is hard, but unless you are willing to lose one of the two, you must learn to find the right balance. Blending your life's focus and the requirements of your job may seem impossible, but if you've clearly defined what's central to your life and are prepared to make sacrifices to achieve it, then making the appropriate adjustments can follow naturally.

You must also be careful not to allow the pursuit of balance to cause dissatisfaction or regret; if you take away effort from the business to dedicate it to family, in the process, you may feel guilty for not putting your best effort in favor of the business.

Here are ways to help you identify your focus, hold yourself accountable, and be successful in your career:

- Define your priorities. What is most important? Is it your business or your family, your business or your health?
- Start by asking yourself three key questions: Where am I? Where do I want to go? How can I get there?
- Define what activities contribute to your goals both at work and in your private life, and then assign priorities to them.

- Make necessary sacrifices. Once you identify your focus, realize that to achieve and maintain it, you'll have to make sacrifices marked by difficult, often life-changing decisions.
- Work is done at work, not at home; only business emergencies should be dealt with at home.
- Set boundaries, and make others aware of them. Once you've established your goals, determine your limits.
- Know your limits. Once you understand what's important to you, decide how much is too much.
- Track your progress. Achieving focus is a process that must be monitored diligently.

Once you determine your priorities, hold yourself accountable to make them happen.

With regards to the culture of accountability, several authors have published steps to create a culture of accountability; the following excerpt is from Victoria Downing (Management Training Systems Inc.):

We all say that we want our people to be accountable and responsible for their actions, but are we doing what it takes to achieve these results? Here are my suggestions for building this culture within your remodeling company:

1. Communicate to everyone that accountability and commitment are important.
2. Align every job description to your company's strategy and goals for the coming year.
3. Make accountabilities clear for everyone by using a benchmark for their job.
4. When you onboard new employees, have job-related professional development resources already in place to help them reach their full potential.
5. Build accountability into your company culture using "what and by when" goal and task planning.

6. Offer ways for employees to communicate obstacles and request the help or resources they need to achieve their goals.
7. Involve employees in an ongoing dialogue about how they can identify process improvements or otherwise increase the quality of their work and the team's productivity.
8. Use small "course corrections" on a monthly or as-needed basis to guide employees toward behaviors and practices that are effective for meeting goals.
9. "Catch" people doing something right: Give frequent, honest, and positive feedback.
10. Identify ways to recognize and acknowledge employees company-wide when their actions exemplify an "above and beyond" commitment to company objectives. Success breeds success.

The next list is from SmallBizClub.com:

1. Clear understanding of what is expected
2. Planning for the unknown
3. Mutually understood consequences
4. Detailed follow-up plan
5. Course correct when needed
6. Be consistent
7. Be involved
8. Assume nothing
9. Recognize performance
10. If success doesn't come, go to right person, right place, and right time

This one is from Accountability Experts Inc.:

1. Clearly define the desired outcome of what you are intending to communicate to the other person or persons.
2. Ask the other person, "How clear is my request on a scale of one to ten?"

3. Allow the other person or persons to participate in some sort of dialogue.
4. Ask people to then play back what they have understood you to say and/or have heard.
5. Depending upon the person you are conversing with, you or the other person may then summarize again to ensure ultra clarity before moving forward.
6. Set timelines. Without timelines in the accountability process, we really have nothing.
7. Be sure to ask what help and/or resources others need from you and/or your company to ensure completion of the requested item.
8. Check-Ins. Between the start of the requested outcome and the committed timeframe of completion, be sure to touch base with the person(s) to best insure they are on schedule.
9. Close the loop. What are you going to do to best ensure accountability?
10. What to do. What happens if your request for the desired outcome is not achieved by this person on time?

Finally, John Stoker offers ten tips to include when creating a company culture:

1. Invite perspective
2. Be patient
3. Listen for what's important
4. Don't push your point of view
5. Take your time
6. Gently challenge assumptions and negative projections
7. Don't assume anything
8. Don't take things personally
9. Offer support
10. Thank others for sharing

All the above comments can be summarized into these ideas:

- encourage clear communication
- open a line of dialogue
- involve your employees
- reward your employees

Linda Galindo says that creating accountability in an organization is a three-part process:

- responsibility
- self-empowerment
- personal accountability

Empowering employees involves distributing the power of decision making, discretion, and resources to subordinates. Empowerment contributes to the performance of an organization because it motivates employees, and motivated employees produce more. When you assign work to others, you are empowering them to own the work, and when they assume responsibility for a project, they are self-empowered to make it happen. The owner of the work doesn't let roadblocks get in the way of seeing things through to a successful completion. To be able to empower yourself, you must be clear in what is expected about the project and what is expected of the owner; without this knowledge, you risk failing because of missed requirements. If clear expectations are not given, you should demand them or decline responsibility for the project.

As you assume responsibility and self-empowerment, you also assume accountability. You are accountable for the successful or unsuccessful completion of the work you do. There are no excuses in your language. You can't assign blame to anybody or anything; you take the fall when something fails, and you do a self-assessment of what went wrong. You do a postmortem analysis and make the necessary corrections or adjustments to ensure it won't happen again. The organization must eliminate words and terms such as "I'll try," "I can't say for sure," "I won't be able to," "That's not my job," "I didn't have the tools," "I had no support," "That's not my [or our] fault," and all other terms that express negativity, doubt, and covering oneself.

Requirements to establish a culture of accountability:

- Give employees the freedom for to say no.
- Inspect what you expect and support your employees.
- Eliminate wiggle room.
- Keep your word.
- Don't settle for dreams and wishes.
- Overcommitment is not commitment at all.
- Objectives without action plans are just dreams.
- To exist without limits is to act without values.
- The pursuit of mediocrity is almost always successful.
- What you accept is what you teach.
- Practice tough love.

Organizations that value personal accountability have employees

- who offer to help achieve goals and objectives and avoid placing blame on others,
- who look for ways to adapt to change and communicate better with others in the organization,
- who work to meet deadlines and established timelines,
- who recognize that creative means to solve problems must be used to make up for this absence of unlimited resources, and
- who believe in and support the mission, vision, and values of the organization.

Takeaways from Chapter 4

- No truly successful organization can do without personal accountability as a core value.
- Personal accountability starts at the top.
- Personal accountability is not a trait that people are born with; it is a way of living and acting that you can learn.

- Personal accountability is what makes individuals do what it takes to achieve the goals and desired outcomes while complying with policies.
- Accountability is not something you make people do; you must create the culture and have people buy into the concept.
- Accountability is a synonym of responsibility and the opposite of permissiveness.
- Balancing life and business is hard, but unless you are willing to lose one of the two, you must learn to find the right balance.
- To be able to empower yourself, you must be clear in what is expected about the project and what is expected of the owner.
- Create a culture of accountability.

CHAPTER FIVE
ACCOUNTABILITY AND LEADERSHIP

What You Accept Is What You Teach

While everyone is accountable for their own behavior, leaders are ultimately responsible for employee performance and therefore are accountable for that. By setting their own standards of exceptional performance, leaders teach employees to be accountable for their own actions and attitudes. To exist without limits is to act without values; leaders must establish boundaries of work performance but also set reasonable standards of conduct. If management is passive and tolerates less-than-ideal behavior, it creates a permissive work environment that can negatively affect the performance of the company.

Accountability is the mark of a true leader; it's a commitment to excellence and shows the will to succeed. True leaders foster ownership and self-motivation among their employees; this leads to greater employee engagement, and for engaged employees, accountability is a personal investment in and ownership of the work they do. It is much easier to cultivate engagement and ownership from the first day of employment of a new member of a team as opposed to retraining to replace accumulated bad practices. To achieve that, management must provide mentorship by being available to reiterate deliverables and align an employee's strengths with the company's goals. Seek feedback by encouraging active participation in meetings and give employees a voice. Encourage coaching of new employees by those already versed in the culture of responsibility and accountability.

What you accept is what you teach. If leaders don't reinforce outstanding performance and hold everyone accountable for it, they are compromising the organization's mission and diminish their own credibility. Marginal employees are reflections of their managers. Great leaders stay true to their values, no matter what the consequences; they believe that betraying their values constitutes a moral failure. By standing firm, they inspire others and transform their organization. Unfortunately, many managers are conflict adverse; because of pressure by a litigious society or by work pressure, some managers lower their standards, tolerate minimum acceptable performance, and settle for mediocre results.

By permitting shoddy performance, leaders (of any level) create a work environment in which less-than-optimum behavior is tolerated. Weak leaders permit complacency and mediocrity of the staff; some are unaware they are doing so, while others are afraid of reprisals or want to be liked instead of respected. Staying their ground and penalizing culprit employees may mean worker turnover; they take the easy road and permit a lack of accountability. Since an employee's performance is a reflection of the leader, it is the leader who ultimately pays the consequences.

Holding people accountable doesn't have to be negative or abusive for the employee; to the contrary, establishing clear goals and helping employees achieve those goals are motivators for the employee and are the essence of effective performance management. When you overlook poor performance from some, you risk losing the respect of many. Most people—all people, I would venture to say—want to see the same rules applied to everyone equally, and they appreciate it when management holds others accountable, as they hold themselves. Good employees would rather be shorthanded for lack of others to help than deal with an incompetent or uncooperative co-worker; by being weak, management risks losing the good employees.

Leaders take personal responsibility; they do what they say and also expect others to do the same. No organization can grow and prosper until its leaders are willing to take responsibility and accept the accountability that goes with it. Without accountability, even the most seemingly qualified leader will fail. Accepting accountability means that they respond to what they do, both good and bad, and they also assume ownership for the performance of their teams (the buck stops at their desk). They instill responsibility in all members of their organization, and since responsibility and accountability go together, they teach and demand accountability.

Too often, leaders of organizations are quick to take credit for successes and avoid responsibility when things don't go right. This behavior will not hold for a true leader because without accountability, there is no effective leadership. Leadership includes the resolution that whatever decision they make, they will assume responsibility, no matter what the outcome; they will take responsibility for the results. Leaders should follow up to evaluate the consequences of their decisions, and if the outcomes are not yielding the desired results, they must make the necessary corrections. Leaders must be accountable, as leaders and as individuals.

Sadly, of all the things that are expected of leaders, accountability is something few people excel in. Despite what many managers and people in leadership claim, most don't know how to hold subordinates accountable. Why is this? Overfield and Kaiser claim that "when it comes to hold[ing] people's feet to the fire, leaders step back from the heat." In their research, they found that almost half of the large number of people they interviewed scored low in holding people accountable, and they say this is true for all levels of management. In my experience with coaching hundreds of CEOs and executives, I also found this to be true. In fact, many of the CEOs I worked with admitted this fault and embraced my practice of holding them accountable and teaching them how to hold their people accountable.

I believe that this somewhat peculiar thing has become more pronounced with the immersion of the younger generation (Generation Y and millennials) into the workforce. These groups expect praise and recognition and can be indignant when they don't receive it; some managers choose to prevent that reaction by omitting criticism and therefore not teaching or demanding accountability. Overfield and Kaiser also claim that another reason for the reluctance to demand accountability is that typically in working groups, there are what they call "free-riders" who don't carry their own weight, depending instead on the work of others. They enjoy the benefits of the working group without making contributions to it; consequently, accountability doesn't count for them. We see then that developing accountability is a challenge for most leaders, particularly young leaders and those just assuming a leadership position.

Responsible employees do the work, but accountable employees find meaning in the work because they own the work. They also understand how their work is connected to the goals of the organization and why what they do is so important. Conversely, when leaders don't promote responsibility and accountability, they are overshadowed in the long run by the creation of a culture of mediocrity and poor performance. If this culture expands throughout the organization, its cost to the organization can be staggering.

For leaders to become more accountable, they must start with honesty; set aside personal pride and admit mistakes by being completely honest. They must also learn to say, "I'm sorry," when something goes wrong, and it is their responsibility. But words only are not sufficient; they must focus on making amends. They must also set pride aside and be willing to seek help from others about why the fault happened and how it could have been prevented. Of course, leaders cannot avoid responsibility and must avoid overpromising and under-delivering, but they must be true to whatever they commit to do. In short, accountability in leadership makes a difference in the business. They must avoid not following through with the process of self-discipline in accountability because this can cause a loss of respect from employees who question their commitment, undermining the whole organization.

The three most important decisions leaders must make are who they hire, who they promote, and who they allow to remain on their team. Leaders are only as good as the team they manage, and unless they have the best players in the most strategic positions, the team will never realize its full potential. Therefore, management must hire strategically, selecting personalities that will adapt to the accountability culture of the company. Thereafter, management must sharpen skills to reward and penalize appropriately and according to the needs of the company; this may require decisions that are complicated and unpleasant but necessary to the well-being of the organization. And if an employee lacks the will or skills to perform the job effectively, management must highlight performance deficiencies with the aim to correct them, without making the employee feel less valuable.

Some employees may have never received an honest appraisal in their life; no manager has ever leveled with them and made them see where their performance needs improvement. By this lack of action from managers, they have been conditioned to think that their performance is acceptable, thus creating a problem for coworkers with their counterproductive behavior and for customers who are victims of the poor quality products they receive. The employees who are held accountable for poor performance don't cause as much trouble as those who are not held accountable but should be. Valuable employees will question why they should work hard and perform admirably when poor performers remain on the team. Good employees do not enjoy working with toxic coworkers and may elect to leave rather than accept this injustice. Overlooking the misbehavior of a few, management risks losing the respect of many, and if poor performers are kept because of personnel shortages, management will create a toxic environment and cause severe damage to the organization.

Tough Love in Leadership

In business, as in other areas of our lives, in order to achieve balance, and ultimately success, we need to have oppositional forces present and equal. As leaders, it is important when dealing with employees to focus on the combination of seemingly opposing forces: tough love. Leaders must believe and practice tough love with employees to be effective in their role. The key is to know in what proportion each part will be applied. If there is too much of one or the other, the leader becomes an ineffective manager.

The hard part is being vigilant in the pursue of excellence and having the courage to demand the best of subordinates. True leaders are not reluctant to exercise the power inherent in being the leader without being afraid to hurt someone's feelings, to achieve positive results through ethical means. If leaders are reluctant to enforce excellence for fear of not being liked, they may end up not being liked or respected by employees. Leaders are accountable when managing an organization, and if the work team they manage fails to adhere to accepted standards of conduct, service, or production, they will lose their leadership position.

Employees know when their leader believes in them, is vested in their success, and will strive to help them meet lofty expectations. Leaders should support employees under fire, provide resources for them, and remove systems barriers that could impede their success. This support does not mean unconditional acceptance of everything the employees do; that could compromise a leader's standards and values. Leaders should remind employees that while they are sensitive to a worker's situation and feelings, their main responsibility and priority is to make sure that the work gets done. They will hold all employees accountable for their conduct and their contributions to the organization.

If the tough part is greater, the leader is classified as a jerk, unfair, or even worse adjectives and end up with poorly performing employees who are overstressed and unhappy. Even more damaging is that they will be afraid of the leader's next tantrum. Conversely, when the leader shows too much love, there is no accountability, which means no positive results. However, combining the two oppositional traits, tough love opens up the path to success. Effective leadership involves the artful combination of these seemingly conflicting approaches. It's not easy to master this delicate balance, but if it's done right, it can be the driving force of a leader and result in employee progress.

Being tough doesn't mean being demanding or aggressive; it just means being assertive and confronting tough problems head-on. When employees realize that the leader has their best interest in mind, they won't question the motives when they get direct feedback; they'll embrace the input. Furthermore, if team members feel that the leader believes in them, they won't complain about the accountability measures imposed on them. Accountability measures become a way for them to assess their goals and provide their own tracking of what was met and what wasn't.

When it's clear that those measures are intended to help them improve, employees will be willing to do what they can to help themselves. They will also accept more demanding tasks in the name of their own personal growth; the leader and the organization will benefit with the added bonus of personal and team accountability. When things don't happen the way they should, enact the accountability measures; when you promise something for a goal achieved, stand by that. When employees trust their leader, they'll be more willing to stake their career goals on the company.

With accountability, good leaders set high standards for the work but implement them with good reason; they don't assign more work or more stringent measures just to justify leadership. Make sure employees know that expectations are high and that their output will be judged accordingly. Make sure the logic behind a task or a work assignment is explained in detail so that all team members involved buy in to its importance. If they don't, it will never be completed to the level the leader desires.

Tough love means being hard and soft at the same time. It's a combination of honest feedback, setting challenging objectives and standards, and being encouraging and empowering. Managers should be critical of their team in private and supportive in public (use the mirror and window approach discussed in the next chapter). A team member will always appreciate a leader who is hard but fair and looks out for employees and their well-being. Tough love is the fastest way to building trust and getting results. Leaders have responsibility for the growth and development of their teams;

therefore, setting high demands while still being supportive is the way to achieve goals and improve team performance.

Tough love actually requires empowerment and includes the leader's conviction that the employee can perform better. Applying tough love includes a hidden message that the person can do better.

Rules of Tough Love Leadership

- Judge employees for their behavior, not for their personality. In order for employees to take criticism in a constructive way, they should be judged on their behavior. If you don't give personal feedback, it will not be taken personally.
- The leader's role is that of guiding the employee without necessarily demonstrating superiority.
- Set challenging but realistic goals; use SMART goals.
- Be clear about goals but remain flexible about the way they are achieved. Set challenging objectives, and make sure the team understand its values and the company's values. Encourage the team to reach those goals rather than guard them each step of the way.
- When the goals are understood by employees, help them with coaching and listen for suggestions, but refrain from micromanaging.
- Tough love goes both ways; you need to provide honest feedback, but you must also be ready to receive it.

Some bosses fire nonperforming employees at their first fault, impose unyielding standards, and manage with the belief that their word is law. With tough love, the challenge is to set high demands while still being supportive. Employees will accept the challenge, and they'll thrive. On the other hand, fear should never be a primary motivator, as employees won't respond to it; even if they try, they won't perform as expected. Indeed, managers who exert too much toughness and not enough love might discover some unintended consequences. To be a leader, you sometimes have to be the bad guy and give up any dreams of being adored by employees. If that sounds tough, it is.

In *QBQ: The Question behind the Question,* John Miller says that a leader should ask the following:

- What action can I take today to contribute?
- How can I help solve the problem?
- What risk can I engage in that will lead me to personal growth?
- How can I do my job in the best possible way?
- What good stuff can I get done before lunch?

He also adds a few tidbits:

- It's better to be one who is told to wait than one who waits to be told.
- Lack of initiative today may guarantee lack of employment tomorrow.
- Taking action may seem risky, but doing nothing is a bigger risk.

In *What Is Leadership?,* Ulrich and Smallwood tell us that leaders build accountability in others and for themselves through four principles:

- Take personal responsibility. Resist the urge to blame others and adopt a mind-set of personal responsibility as a leader.
- Go public. When leaders go public with their goals, they are more likely to achieve them.
- Be consistent with your personal values and brand. Value consistency helps leaders to think and act with continuity so their stance and actions are clear to both themselves and observers.
- Hold others accountable. Sustainable leadership occurs when others are accountable.

The view of leadership must be transmitted throughout the organization and be consistent with the values of the leader. Leaders need to be conscious of how their style affects others and adjust it accordingly. Again, quoting Ulrich and Smallwood, consistent leadership happens when others are accountable, and they can drive accountability in others by

- setting clear objectives,
- identifying measures,
- ensuring consequences, and
- providing ongoing feedback and follow-up.

Clear objectives are necessary to judge success (or the lack of it). Individual competencies and results as well as team results must be measured, and the consequences, both positive and negative, must be applied. Feedback is important because without it, employees will lack accountability; they won't have the opportunity to learn from their mistakes and change their behavior. There are informal ways that leaders can measure accountability in an organization; for example, they can meet with customers, suppliers, and others to see how they feel about the organization. They must listen carefully to what they hear. For these interactions to have validity, leaders must build credibility by having them regularly.

An accountable leader must lead from the front, be self-accountable, and make effective contributions to the organization. This sense of accountability is one of the most vital things for a leader as an individual and as the one responsible for the organization. Effective leadership includes giving employees the opportunity to hold themselves accountable, take responsibility, and be part of the team. Leaders should take every accountability occasion as a learning opportunity, and after gathering all the facts, they should also ask themselves what was the takeaway from the incident and what they learned from it.

Clarity Is Key and Starts with You

Ambiguity is the enemy of accountability. Many problems with accountability stem from a failure to create a high level of clarity in what tasks are to be done, what team members are responsible for, and details that are paramount to the completion of the jobs. Accountability means little if specific goals are not clearly communicated. Not knowing exactly what to do, how results are to be measured, and what results are expected can be frustrating for employees; unclear marching orders can be exasperating and demoralizing, but it gets worse when after finishing the job, the leader tells them, "That's not what I wanted."

The instructions to be given at the time of assigning the job should include the expected outcome, when it should be completed, what actions are to be taken upon completion, and other management expectations. Targets and metrics must be well defined and include limits of measurements, remembering that you can't manage what you can't measure.

Employees should speak up and demand clear instructions and expectations; they should not be exposed to blaming or finger-pointing. If everyone acts this way, it forces the culture to develop accountability, and that becomes the way it's done. Although this is critical to success, few companies encourage it. Required times of completion must be realistic, and sufficient resources must be available. If the project is long or extensive, progress should be reviewed periodically to make sure the work is on track. These reviews should be scheduled at the time of the assignment, and the schedules should be kept religiously; otherwise, you send the message that they are not important.

We often assume that we have been perfectly clear in our verbal instructions, and we also assume that tacit acknowledgments from employee is proof that the message was received. This false sense of security can lead to performance breakdowns. Because of this, it is highly recommended that all instructions be given in writing and that the recipient fully understands them and accepts them. This will also prevent disagreements on performance issues, which can also create serious employee-employee or employee-management disputes. Writing clarifies thinking, helps to confirm understanding with others, and saves time and expense by avoiding project rework and restarts.

Written agreements are not usually needed for routine tasks, for simple projects, or with people who are known to deliver on their commitments, but they are critical tools when transmitting instructions for complex projects, new tasks, specialized tools, and new personnel. Furthermore, these written instructions become de facto contracts that can be beneficial in cases of disputes or conflicts. Written agreements make things stated rather than assumed and forces everyone to accept responsibility before the project begins.

The written agreements—de facto contracts—must be negotiable, and management must allow employees to question certain conditions and even say no when the situation warrants it. For example, adding new assignments to an already overflowing slate of tasks can tax the stress level of employees and endanger the quality of work, risking a loss in what they are expected to accomplish. When a reasonable agreement is negotiated, when people have clear guidelines, and when they are empowered, the excuses are eliminated, the work gets done, and people stay motivated.

Team Accountability

When projects are assigned to a team, its leader is accountable for the team's overall performance. It is typical in this case to give the instructions to the leader; however, the entire team should ideally receive the same instructions. When this is the case, it gives all team members the opportunity (and obligation) to hold each other accountable for their performance. The team leader assumes full responsibility and accountability, but without absolving team members of their own self-empowerment and accountability. Moreover, the team as a whole may be held accountable for meeting the expected targets.

My Experience

A sport analogy can be used to illustrate this concept. I used to coach youth soccer teams (luckily, with great success). However, one time after we lost a game, I heard a lot of players blame the goalie for not stopping the goals, the fullbacks for not preventing the other team from shooting, and the forwards for not scoring themselves. I was naturally disappointed, not at the lost game but at the attitude of the players. I had a frank and severe talk with the team, explaining that everyone was responsible for the work of the team and, therefore, accountable for the loss. Naturally, I did not escape my own criticism and explained that as the leader of the team, I was responsible for the game strategy I had formulated and accountable for not correcting it as the game proceeded. I made them understand that while everyone was responsible and accountable for their own performance, I had the lion's share of the accountability. It was a lesson I hoped they did not forget.

There are times when a lack of accountability within a team leads to unfair recognition among the team members; in other words, it may lead to equal rewards for unequal performance. When this happens, high-performance individuals may see no value in working hard to achieve the goals of the team. This can lead to resentment, bad relations within the team, and lower performance. Measurement of performances is critical and must be fairly applied to all. Unless there are good measurements, employees will not prosper, and high achievers will feel unappreciated. They are likely to leave. To retain high achievers, everyone must be held accountable.

My Experience

I was an active participant in another example. A new company in the semiconductor industry was struggling to reach acceptable yields, despite their concentrated efforts. There were several departments responsible for different segments of the complicated manufacturing process, and it wasn't easy to identify the contributions of each department in the overall yields. Not unexpectedly, there was a significant amount of finger-pointing between departments, with most claiming innocence and producing data that they claimed confirmed it, while pointing to other process segments as the culprits. This went on for a long time without being resolved, and as a consequence, the company failed to meet its goal of entering the market. Had the culture of the company emphasized team accountability, the various departments would have worked together to solve the quality issues, and the company would have succeeded.

In *The Five Dysfunctions of a Team,* Patrick Lencioni says that "ambiguity is the enemy of accountability." Many problems with accountability originate from a failure to create a level of clarity around tasks and not from inherently irresponsible or unqualified employees. Lencioni identifies the avoidance of accountability as one of the five dysfunctions, but in reality, analyzing them carefully, all five dysfunctions are related to accountability. According to the book, these are the five dysfunctions:

- Absence of trust: unwilling to be vulnerable within the group
- Fear of conflict: seeking artificial harmony over constructive passionate debate
- Lack of commitment: feigning buy-in for group decisions, creating ambiguity throughout the organization
- Avoidance of accountability: ducking the responsibility to call peers on counterproductive behavior that sets low standards
- Inattention to results: focusing on personal success, status, and ego before team success

Lencioni defines *accountability* as "the willingness of team members to remind one another when they are not living up to the performance standards of the group." By this definition, it seems simple to just get team members to remind one another of their issues, but in reality, we must work through barriers presented by personalities, jealousy, ambition, and drive to get team members to work together.

It may be easy in some cases but not so easy in others; the talents of a leader are put to the test to accomplish that. It cannot be done in one day; it takes quite some time and a lot of patience.

My Experience

In my business coaching activities, I worked with a company that was going through some difficult times with internal friction; team members blamed each other for problems. Individually, all members were excellent contributors because of their technical capabilities, but as a team, they were not functioning for the betterment of the enterprise. I followed Lencioni's teaching and attacked the problem as a function of the lack of team accountability. Individual members were preoccupied with their own individual performance and passing blame for poor team performance.

Working with each member individually and with the team as a group, including the CEO, I identified the main reason for the problem: a perception that rules were not applied equally to all members; some felt they were being treated unfairly. We had several wide-open, frank discussions, and I instructed the CEO to judge each member individually and demonstrate equal treatment to the team. It wasn't easy and, at times, was uncomfortable, but they were able to see their faulty behavior and committed to correcting the situation. Following it with personal coaching for each member, the environment changed drastically, and the company started to function in admirable form.

In another situation, the general manager of a division created an uncomfortable environment by giving low grades to employees who, in his judgment, had not performed to expectations. Unfortunately, his expectations were unreasonable; he had not provided the tools and training the people needed to perform the job. In addition, he was at fault for not holding himself accountable; he tried to blame the employees for not performing. As his coach, I had to have some difficult sessions with him to make him realize his faults. To his credit (and mine), he finally realized his shortcomings and made an effort to correct the situation. This resulted in a major improvement in the performance and camaraderie within the division.

It is interesting that many business owners seem ignorant about accountability and don't know how to implement a culture of accountability in their companies. Consequently, in my work with peer advisory boards, I developed a training process designed to educate executives on the importance of a system of accountability. This process became a staple in my training program, and members perceived it as a key value of belonging to the boards. It simply consisted of having them develop sets of goals, both personal and business, and having the board of peers hold each other accountable for meeting those goals. Monthly reviews of the goals usually generated very valuable discussions.

Holding team members accountable or driving them to be accountable can be a challenging interaction; these conversations have the potential for strong emotions. These conversations require courage because they can jeopardize the quality of relationships with coworkers. But if team members choose not to meet a commitment, they hurt themselves but also the team and, likely, the entire organization. For some employees, holding others accountable may mean (in their eyes) pointing fingers and accusing teammates; thus, they don't want to be known as betraying a team member's loyalty. The leader should hold the team accountable for holding each other accountable.

Organizations must teach that holding others accountable is not about blaming them or finding fault or accusing them or saying what they should have done; it is about expecting the best from coworkers but also offering help to achieve the goals. In fact, holding others accountable can help build stronger relationships, if done right. The challenge is to convince them that accountability means something totally different; it means teamwork and working together toward a common goal. Personal credibility and pride of achievement are gained through accountability.

The process is not about finding fault or accusing others of what they should have done; it's about helping them improve for their own betterment and the betterment of the team and the organization.

Written agreements related to the project at hand keeps the focus on goals previously agreed to and eliminates such arguments as "I didn't know" or "I thought it was better this way." By dealing with gaps between the agreement and the actual results, the discussion becomes as objective as possible. Furthermore, by providing suggestions about fixes that can be applied in the future and offering to help implement them, it becomes a pleasant exchange and a win-win scenario for all involved.

Team members must understand that they are responsible for continuous improvement; in order to grow their skills, they must be open to trying new ideas and investigating various solutions to known problems. Employees should be encouraged to be aware of how they influence the work environment by how they perform and even how they choose the words they use. Too many times, they respond to a challenge using words that reflect negatively on the team. Phrases such as "I'll try my best," "I can't say for sure," and "I won't promise" should be replaced with "I will," "I can," and "I'm sure." It is important to coach employees on how to use the correct words and explain how the wrong words affect the work environment.

Chapter 5 Takeaways

While everyone is accountable for their own behavior, leaders are ultimately responsible for employee performance and therefore are accountable for it.

- What you accept is what you teach. If you accept mediocrity, you are teaching that mediocrity is acceptable.
- Of all the things that are expected of leaders, the one that few excel in is accountability.
- Responsible employees do the work, but accountable employees find meaning in the work because they own the work.
- The three most important decisions leaders must make are who they hire, who they promote, and who they allow to remain on their team.

- As leaders, it is important to focus on tough love when dealing with employees.
- Tough love is a seemingly opposing combination of honest feedback, setting challenging objectives and standards, and at the same time encouraging and empowering team members.
- Ambiguity is the enemy of accountability. Clarity is key, and it starts at the top.
- If the project is assigned to a team, its leader is accountable for the overall performance of the team.
- Many business owners are ignorant about accountability and don't know how to implement a culture of accountability in their companies.
- Holding team members accountable can be a challenging interaction because these conversations have the potential for strong emotions.
- Organizations must teach that holding others accountable is about teaching and offering help to achieve the goals.

CHAPTER SIX
IMPLEMENTATION

The Process of Implementation

In teaching accountability, you need to stress the importance of written agreements and clarify how they are negotiated. The agreement must be like a contract, specifying very clearly the when and how of the job in a way that leaves no room for misunderstanding; every employee must realize the commitment they are making. Remember that this is a contract, and as such, both parties have a right to discuss its contents and to only agree to what they believe is fair. Listen carefully to the other side, understand their position, and make sure there is mutual agreement for the final version.

You also need to make it culturally acceptable for employees to say no when the situation warrants it. Do they believe that the assignment is not realistic? Do they feel they have too much on their plate already, and you are trying to add more? Are the conditions right for the assignment? Are the goals SMART? Don't force them to sign a contract they don't believe in; the outcome will likely be a failure to meet the objectives and a disgruntled workforce. Accountability results from a system composed of three elements: clarity of the assignment, commitment by both parties, and consequences for the outcome. If you remove the commitment part from the employees, the system breaks down.

My Experience

In my work with a manufacturing company in the high-tech industry (with $27 million in revenues), it was painfully obvious that execution was lacking throughout the organization. As a manufacturer, it had the historical silos of sales, operations, engineering, financial, and supporting functions, with the unfortunate characteristic of not working in unison and employing the typical finger-pointing system.

The company had a target of becoming ISO 9000 certified, so we used this goal as the vehicle to instill teamwork and develop an actionable execution plan that included individual responsibilities and expectations to hold people accountable. We succeeded in both goals, achieving ISO certification in record time and simultaneously creating a culture of execution and accountability that everyone was proud of. And because they saw the benefits, they adopted teamwork and team accountability as their operating mode. This is an example of marrying two goals to achieve a global goal that significantly improved profitability and created a culture of success.

I worked with another organization led by a dictatorial new manager the CEO had hired to shape up the company. This manager demanded employees work on weekends to execute jobs that he wanted to complete on a certain schedule, according to a plan he developed without anybody else's input. The logical unhappiness among employees had a number of negative effects.

He lost the respect of employees (or never had it); some key employees were unable to work under those conditions and left, and the company's culture deteriorated. The remaining employees were very unhappy and—coincidentally—failed to achieve the goals. There was no ownership of the job or tasks, and as a result, there was no individual or team responsibility. Without them, there could be no accountability, resulting in a serious drop in productivity. Fortunately, I convinced the CEO, who realized his mistake and fired the manager, but it took him a long time to rebuild the organization's culture.

When setting goals for a team, stages of development should be based on specific milestones or benchmarks on the way to ultimate completion. Guidelines should be established for team members to report to supervisors at defined steps of the planning or implementation. These reviews steps must be held at predetermined times, and the schedule must be strictly adhered by employees and management; not doing so sends a message that the reviews—and therefore the project—are not important.

When a team is responsible for a project, the team leader must be accountable for its success and timely completion. The leader should report to supervisors and act as a liaison between supervisors and team members. Management should meet with the team prior to the start of the project to establish goals, methods and schedules. The leader should be designated at this point, and all members should recognize their ultimate responsibility and corresponding accountability. Conversely, the leader must keep each member informed of progress and remind them of their individual accountability.

My Experience

Many years ago, when I was working at a large company, the general manager of a division assessed my employees with very low grades because the division had not performed according to expectations. I believed that his decision was unfair because the department I managed had excelled in our performance; we surpassed our goals and thus did not deserve the low classification. I thought that he as the leader of the division should be accountable for the lack of progress caused by other groups within the division. Needless is to say, my argument was not well received. Nevertheless, I still feel that in such a case, the leader should be accountable to upper management, but group members who excelled in their performance and assumed individual and team accountability themselves should not be penalized.

Metrics are important, but they sometimes drive unexpected behaviors. Wrong measurements or measuring the wrong things can have implications in accountability; therefore, it is important to remember to inspect what you expect, and inspect the right things.

When you set expectations, be sure to eliminate any possibility of misunderstanding. By being specific and putting things in writing, you will prevent disputes, reduce antagonism among team members, and avoid disrespect toward you. A manager who does not establish boundaries by upholding reasonable standards inevitably invites chaos and creates a permissive environment in which bad behaviors are tolerated or even encouraged.

Not everything that counts can be counted, and not everything that can be counted counts. This axiom is particularly true when it refers to accountability. Measurements applicable to accountability are basically those things that are expected in the performance of the job, things such as quantities produced, the time it took to produce them, dimensions obtained, date of completion, quality-related factors, reports produced, the number of words in a book or memo, and everything that was part of the specifications when the job was assigned and the responsibility accepted by the employee. Measurements not related to the job may be important for other reasons but are not necessarily pieces of the accountability diagram.

Make only promises that you intend to keep. Keep your word; whatever you say is taken as the word from the top, and it is expected to be true. Your team members should not hold themselves more accountable than you hold yourself. When employees first hear the word *accountability*, they often wince, thinking it's another name for punishment. By openly holding yourself accountable, you are dissipating that belief. Remind everyone that a commitment is much more than "I'll try." Practice tough love to be an effective manager. Always be vigilant in the pursuit of excellence; display no favoritism, serve as a role model, and provide recognition to others for achievements. An objective without a plan is just a dream, and dreams are not real commitments or promises at all, just wishes in disguise. The plan to reach an objective must be real and believed by all. It should provide the opportunity to measure progress and predict the end. Many objectives are never achieved because no one ever planned to achieve them, even if there were good intentions.

Make sure that a team's objective is not in opposition with the objectives of another team. One member's success should not result in another member's failure. Have members work with each other and check for conflicts, and be prepared to confront those who shy away from such confrontations. Require team members to take their complaints to each other and not just come complaining to you. Encourage them to compliment each other for success. Don't allow them to approve everything you say just because you are their boss; encourage them to challenge you if they believe they have a valid point. You will gain a lot of insight by doing this.

Never wait until just before a deadline is reached to check on the progress of a project. Once the project is behind schedule, it's too late to do anything about it, and whatever help you offer at that time will not be effective. Celebrate triumphs. If the project is finished on time and in the manner originally planned, make sure you take time to celebrate. Let the team know publicly that it did a great job, but make sure you do it fairly and without making others who also may have performed well feel any less successful. Giving lots of positive attention to this kind of work habit and behavior will help to create a culture of accountability for everyone in the organization. Everyone will start holding each other accountable, and you will be well on your way to creating a culture of accountability.

Nordstrom is an excellent example of accountability in action. The company encourages salespeople to use their initiative to deliver exceptional customer service, and it rewards them for taking the lead in satisfying customers. It gives them freedom to help customers; there is not only one way to do business, and it accepts whatever it takes to make the customer happy. Leaders building high-performance organizations recognize that accountability is a personal trait that must be nurtured; those who look for scapegoats cannot expect their employees to display accountability.

Hiring the right people is critically important, and the right people are willing to be accountable. But in order for them to be consistently accountable, they must be aligned with the organization's vision, mission, and strategies. They must be empowered to take the actions necessary to follow the vision, while being firmly in line with the organization's core values. Empowerment is a must because it's difficult to be accountable if employees are not allowed to take ownership of projects. Conversely, organizations must set clear goals, clarify expectations, and have an accurate way of determining contributing factors and recognizing employee successes.

When people experience the sense of accountability shown by other members, they will be motivated to be more accountable themselves, creating a virtual spiral of attributes such as teamwork and innovation. Those who feel victims drain the organization of cohesiveness and energy, while those who clearly show accountability strengthen the company's positive culture. This difference also motivates individuals to explore personal leadership, and they should be recognized by the organization and their performance rewarded.

Accountability must be pushed to the lowest level in the organization; that is, everyone should be part of the accountability culture, and everyone must be taught accountability. Line workers have pride too, and as such, they should be given responsibilities, offered empowerment, and held accountable, regardless of the complexity of the tasks they perform. All leaders must ask themselves the following questions:

- Am I enforcing accountability to the lowest possible level?
- Am I dealing with this enforcement in an effective way?
- Am I aware of what needs of mine may compromise accountability?
- Am I teaching my subordinates to hold their subordinates accountable?
- Do I have a need to look good to management or to the team?
- Am I pushing for ownership of issues for employees?
- Am I giving authority with responsibility?
- Do I provide adequate resources to my employees?

Leaders, and every member of the organization, must never lose sight of the ultimate goal of the company and of the team. They must minimize status differences, regardless of titles, insist on mutual respect, and reinforce the team concept. Individuals are accountable to the team, and if they are accountable to the leader, he is accountable to the management team. Leaders must set an example and be accountable in all situations while at the same time instilling optimism and self-confidence in their subordinates to be accountable themselves.

Five Tips for Creating More Accountability.

Finding ways to instill accountability in an organization should be the goal of most leaders, and there are many published recommendations for doing it. The American Express Forum published the following list that I find useful:

1. Declare goals publicly. The idea is to share the goals with others, such as coworkers, team members, family, friends, stakeholders, and other witnesses. When you share your goals and proclaim that you will do something, you are more driven to reach your objective.
2. State your planning and share your to-do list. Sharing your plans and list of actions with your team builds trust and forces accountability. If you meet your goals, you will look good to team members and others, and if you miss your target or your colleagues notice that you constantly miss milestones, they will start asking questions and maybe demanding answers.
3. Rewire your approach and stop focusing on short-term rewards. It's much easier to do smaller, easier tasks and get a feeling of accomplishment; people often push back those tasks they don't like or that take more dedication, but by doing this, you may be sacrificing the long-term success of the organization. Rewiring requires finding a way to enjoy the long-term tasks that take you to the ultimate goal. One way to do this is to break down large tasks into smaller pieces

that will allow people to enjoy the short-term rewards of completing each step.
4. Leverage fighting to stay on track. In the work environment, we often try to stay away from arguments or disagreements with coworkers because it's easier to not rock the boat, but productive teams actually encourage healthy arguments, exploring all possible solutions to a given problem. A quick consensus is comfortable, but a vigorous debate moves the team to find the best solution.
5. List out action steps after brainstorming session and impromptu gatherings. When the exhilaration of a good exchange of ideas and plans takes over, we may forget about accountability. To ensure that we capture the valuable ideas, we should record every meeting with all the action items decided on.

My Experience

I worked with a successful manufacturing company that was owned and run by two partners. The senior partner was the administrative and visionary type, while the junior partner was the operations expert. They both developed plans, with the participation of the management team. Execution was the weakest link in this otherwise excellent company. The reason: It lacked a culture of accountability between departments, creating tension, with a focus on covering people's faults; the root source of the problem was that the partner in charge of operations did not impose the discipline of accountability.

What was the solution? This partner could not be fired; he was a talented executive and an owner, so the solution was coaching. I worked for quite some time with the operations expert and also with the entire organization, educating them in the value of personal and group accountability, describing how to optimize it, and explaining how to apply it. The solution was implemented, and the company thrived because of it.

Barriers to Implementing Accountability

- Lack of commitment. The lack of accountability is directly related to a lack of commitment. Boosting the commitment levels of employees makes them feel invested in what they do. Effective organizations have teams where everyone feels they have influence. When people feel they have influence and know their voices are being heard, their investment in their work increases and with it, their commitment. Management must set and communicate a clear vision and direction so employees know what needs to be accomplished and what is expected of them. The commitment level of employees will drastically improve if they know the goals of the organization and believe they are valued for their contribution to the company's overall success.
- Lack of ownership. Empowerment is a critical component of accountability, and it follows that one of the greatest barriers to accountability is when people feel they have no control over their work. When employees are empowered and feel in control of a decision, their ownership and accountability skyrockets. Conversely, if they feel that others are in control of how their work gets done, accountability decreases. Simply put, for people to be responsible, they must be clear about the results they are expected to deliver, and then they must have control over how they deliver them.
- Lack of resilience. Resilient employees are given the chance to work through difficult problems and have a safe environment where failure is not penalized; it's understood to be part of the learning process. To increase the resiliency of employees, they must have training in technical competencies and also problem-solving skills. The organization must provide a safe environment where employees don't fear failure. Let employees set realistic goals and then provide the feedback and training necessary for them to build confidence in their

ability to work through problems and overcome whatever challenges they encounter. Encourage communication and collaboration among all employees.

Removing the Barriers

Accountability takes courage and can be uncomfortable if not implemented correctly. People have pride and see themselves as good at what they do; they often fear that the person holding them accountable won't understand what they do or the conditions in which they work. Pride tends to interfere with their rational judgment and how they evaluate the intentions of others. They don't always buy in to accountability, fearing it's punitive, when actually, it helps raise the bar of everyone's performance.

Holding people to their commitments takes work and effort, but it's a necessary use of time for the good of the organization and its employees. Part of the effort is to review commitments and judge if the commitments were accomplished. Following up with people on their commitments gives the message that their work is important. Avoid negativity, give people the space to show they can do good work, and allow them to grow to their potential.

Employees must believe in themselves and in their ability to own the work and perform it successfully. Help them remove the barriers to employee accountability by modeling behavior that's expected of them, and let them see your commitment, ownership, and resilience through your words and actions. Teach employees to set objectives that are realistic, give them control over their work, and then require them to account for their decisions and actions; that's how they develop resilience. Instill accountability by giving employees the skills and control needed to respond to tough problems, and then, after success is achieved, celebrate the victories.

The positive effects of individual ownership of projects are critical benefits obtained by the organization. When employees—even low-level employees—are authorized to take ownership of a job, they assume full responsibility for that operation and don't let any inconveniences get in the way of successfully completing it. For example, a line worker's operation consists of drilling a hole in a part being manufactured; this is their only responsibility: to drill the hole according to the template they are given. It's a very simple operation that needs to be done correctly. If something fails, it is the operator's responsibility to take whatever correction action is demanded and to inform the supervisor. If these employees don't have the authority to take a specific action in pursuit of their goal, they will look for whoever has the authority to request their assistance and resolve any obstacle. Position-based management and the resulting control management will fade away with self-empowerment.

Building a mind-set of empowerment requires people to balance the ability to help coworkers and other company stakeholders with their own responsibility to the organization and find a happy medium that benefits both sides. The secret to freeing the power of committed employees is for leaders to treat subordinates more like partners; they must delegate the authority if possible within the reality of the work, the capacity of the employee, and the policies of the organization. The ultimate goal, of course, is to eliminate excuses, improve productivity, and increase quality while also strengthening individual and team morale.

To achieve personal accountability, employees must be allowed to own a project and to answer for the outcome. Personal action must take place to complete the task, and to be able to do that, employees need to understand why they are doing what they're doing, what the team is trying to achieve, what results are to be obtained, what standards must be met, and how their responsibilities fit into the long-term plan of the company. They should not be forced to follow authoritative demands from those above them in the chain of command. Employees must believe in the goal being pursued and be part of the success when the goal is achieved. They need milestones and results that can be measured because without measurements, they cannot be held accountable.

In the process, there should be dual feedback: comments from the supervisor to the employee and from the employee to the supervisor. There must be clear communications both ways to prevent misunderstandings and the consequent failure of the task. For example, a high-level manager I used to coach was disillusioned with an employee's lack of accountability; he felt she failed to complete a task in the manner the manager expected. He directed the employee to repeat the task, which not surprisingly was completed with the same result.

This created an uncomfortable situation when the manager reproached the employee, who unhappily complained that she had done as he had asked. When I challenged him about the level and clarity of the instructions he had given the employee, it was obvious that they were not clear at all, and thus the employee was not at fault. His reason for the insufficient directions was, as he put it, "she is a senior employee and should know how to do it." While this may have been true in theory, his dissatisfaction was with the process used and not necessarily with the result obtained, but he had neglected to clearly explain how he wanted the project completed; without a doubt, there was a lack of clear communication between him and the employee.

Implementing Accountability in Your Organization

First, you need to decide if accountability is missing from your organization. John Miller, author of *QBQ: The Question behind the Question*, gives some guidelines in this respect:

- Is there a tendency in your company to assign blame? Is it always someone else's fault? This can be on an individual basis or by departments, as in, "We did it right, but they screwed up."
- Do they find fault with other people's work (as in, "I installed the washer right; if the pipes leak, it's the plumber's fault")?
- Do some employees feel they are victims? Do you hear "Nobody tells us what's going on," or "Why do we have to go through all these changes? We are doing fine without them"?

- Do they use procrastination as a weapon? Do people delay activities or push deadlines further away from the agreed-upon date and justify it by saying, "It doesn't matter because nobody will notice anyway," or "Even if I keep the commitment, I won't get any reward."
- Do they make excuses for their performance by blaming it on incidentals, such as, "How can I get it done when I don't have the right tools," or "It's not my fault; I couldn't get any help from engineering"?
- Do your employees look at work as a burden dropped upon them that they cannot escape from, rather than enjoying what they do? I don't mean to be altruistic, but unless employees show some signs of enjoyment (or at least acceptance) of their job, chances are they will resent being held accountable or working in an environment of accountability.

Okay, now you know that you don't have the accountable organization that you need, so how do you build company-wide accountability?

You need to start by eliminating practices that undermine accountability, such as micromanaging and legislating how activities should be conducted. Then start working on team development; eliminate person-to-person competition, and promote person-to-person assistance. Develop goals in agreement with the strategic plan. These goals will have metrics and schedules to meet, and they will have specific team members responsible for meeting them. As a member of the team, you have goals and measurements to meet too; this is your opportunity to set an example for the rest of the team.

Harassment training doesn't work. "Do it because I say so" doesn't work. Discrimination between people and bullying doesn't work. One-way communication doesn't work. Those practices lack a process to foster healthy relationships between employees and management. Don't tell people what to do; ask them to perform a job, and let them own the project. Take off your boss hat and show that you really care; if you do that, employees will learn to trust you and will feel empowered. When employees take this attitude, morale and productivity will increase, and company performance will increase too.

Expectations must be clear and specific; you cannot hold someone accountable for not reading your mind. They must also be linked to results: "If they are not reached, this is what will happen." Expectations have a reason, and this reason must be explained to whoever is held accountable. Don't order something to be done because you say so; explain the reason for what you are asking people to do. Clearly identify, articulate, and execute the strategies and strategic goals; you will be well positioned to create organizational accountability. Decide what's important in the strategic position, and develop the goals together with the systems that support the goals. Don't overlook problems that may come up; work on them to find the root cause, and work as a team to do it. General George Marshall, in commanding his troops, said, "Don't fight problems, solve them."

My Experience

I coached the vice president of a manufacturing company who frequently created organizational and operational problems because of his lack of clarity in assigning projects. He believed that if he hired someone to do a job, the person "should know what to do without me telling him how"; in other words, he assumed the employee knew how he wanted the job done. For example, he asked a line manager to give him a report on a production schedule, without any instructions. When the manager produced the report, my client said, "That's not what I wanted; go back and do it again." Sure enough, the second version was also not what he wanted, and the third version had the same result. He fired the manager, claiming he was unqualified and didn't know how to follow directions (even though he clearly did not give him any directions).

I had to spend a sizable amount of time coaching him in delegation and accountability, until he learned that people are not mind-readers and if you want them to follow your way of doing something, you need to explain to them what that way is.

Follow these steps for creating a culture of commitment and accountability:

- Make exceptionally clear that accountability and commitment are a requirement of the organization, and emphasize that their individual contributions matter.
- Align every job description to your company's strategy and goals. Ask everyone to commit to a shared vision of results.
- Build a culture of accountability by using "what and by when" goal planning.
- Encourage employees to communicate obstacles and request the resources they need to achieve their goals.
- Motivate employees to identify process improvements or otherwise increase the quality and productivity of their work.
- Catch people doing something right; give frequent, honest, and positive feedback. Recognize and acknowledge employees when their actions exemplify an above-and-beyond commitment to company objectives.

In a company with a culture of accountability, people do what they say they'll do and hold themselves and each other accountable. To this end, they must set clearly defined results. These can be sales numbers, profit levels, ROI, positioning in the industry, or any other goal that's part of the strategic plan. Once these goals are set, make sure that the entire organization is clear in what the goals mean for its success and how each employee can affect them. Now develop measurements for each employee or department, implementing joint accountability. Make it clear that "close to the target" is not good enough and that each objective is based on the overall strategy of the company. This mind-set can only become part of the culture if people understand the results they are supposed to achieve in their job.

Joint accountability means that even if individuals have met their goals, if the team hasn't, success has not been achieved. Individual success does not necessarily transmit to group success. Granted, individual accountability must be a reality before joint accountability can be reached, but you must promote both if you are to win the accountability battle. Good managers practice "the mirror and the window," as described by Jim Collins, meaning that when something fails, look into what you could have done wrong (the mirror), and when something succeeds, publicly proclaim the success of the team (the window).

The Difficult Part: How to Correct a Lack of Accountability

What can you do as a leader when a staff member's accountability falters? Everyone wants to excel and be proud of what they do and how they do it, but it's not uncommon to try to cut corners or do only what's necessary to avoid being penalized. That's where accountability plays a role.

Accountability results from an interlocking system of three elements: clarity, commitment, and consequences. We have already stated that to have accountability, there must be consequences, but it's worth repeating it here. There should be consequences for success and consequences for failure. The consequences for success are easy; the grades for failure are more difficult and depend on the ranking of the culprits and the severity of the fault. It can range from a simple verbal admonition to dismissal, but it must be applied fairly, and the reason and punishment must be known by all as a consequence of nonaccountability.

In my personal experience, it always worked for me to simply say, "That's not acceptable," or "That's not the way we do it here," in a firm but gentle way that left no possibility to be taken as just a friendly reminder. This easy approach may not work in every case, and managers or supervisors need to adapt the reproach used to the person given to, the reason of the reproach, and the circumstances. Next, you must take steps to make sure the incident isn't repeated.

Follow the main rule of the International Standards Organization: "Say what you do, and do what you say."

To set up consequences, management must know the people involved; what motivates them? Is it money, promotions, recognition, opportunities to learn? What do they consider success or failure? Consequences for success may include intangibles such as praise, gratitude, recognition, celebrations, and increased levels of responsibility and freedom to act, or tangibles such as rewards, promotions, bonuses, and raises. Consequences of failure may include emotional components such as team disappointment, letting colleagues down, tough conversations or postmortems about what happened, and erosion of trust, and material penalties such as failure to obtain bonuses, raises, or promotions; limited opportunities for desirable assignments; and discipline or possible termination.

If a teammate fails to keep a commitment, it affects the entire team because the team was counting on that promise. Your dilemma in this case is, do you punish the team, or do you punish the individual? My answer is both, because while the individual's nonperformance affected the team, the team failed to hold each member accountable. If you don't act, or worse yet, if you reward the culprit because after all, he did his job, you can count on the incorrect behavior to be repeated. Also remember that there should be consequences for the leader as well.

My Experience

One of my favorite clients was the CEO of a distribution company with approximately $20 million in revenues. He was (and still is) an excellent manager and formed a valuable team of executives in various disciplines. Although the company was doing fine, the CEO was not satisfied because goals were not met, and there was certain disconnect within the team.

We proceeded to do an exercise related to the five dysfunctions of a team, and it became clear that the problem was lack of individual and team accountability, which affected relationships within the team.

After intensive training and coaching, both at the personal level and as a team (including the CEO), the group started to function much better, and the results of the company also improved. The coaching included behavioral assessments and discussions, so the drastically different personalities in the group could understand each other better. As an added bonus, the morale of the group also improved significantly.

But before you think about punishments, consider remedies; what system failed? What part of the training didn't yield the results that it should have? What was your role in the failure? Were the instructions given perfectly clear? Did everyone understand the goals and measurements? Does everyone embrace the team concept? Look into your practices, and assess your role. Reemphasize training and education at all levels. Have a meeting to discuss why it happened, and get everyone's input as to why it won't happen again.

In one-on-ones with employees who do not meet commitments, let them know they are not being accountable. Find out why the failure occurred and how they plan to make it up; offer your help to implement whatever corrective action is needed, and commit to coaching them further in the subject. Be clear on what further consequences will be if the incident is repeated, for whatever reason. Set up frequent review dates for ongoing projects; help employees positively reinforce their successes, and then make the check-in times less and less frequent as accountability improves.

Learn about employees' personalities and characters to see if there is something that makes accountability difficult for them. Are they someone who is unable or unwilling to meet the requirements of the job? Make sure employees are in the right job and have the right responsibilities; many times, workers are asked to perform at a higher level than their capabilities would suggest. The opposite may also be true; asking employees to do menial jobs well below their capabilities may be taken as an insult or a lack of confidence. Make sure, too, that employees are not suffering from demotivation due to extraneous circumstances.

It is important that employees have all the right tools and resources. Until those questions are clarified and the shortfalls are pointed out, you'll never know whether they are unable, unmotivated, or simply in need of help. Consider naming a mentor to work with employees with accountability issues. Help them understand that accountability is an opportunity and not a punishment. If there is a team failure, understand that consequences for employees also have consequences for the leader. The team leader failed to hold members accountable, and thus the leader is at fault too. And if you are the leader of the failing team, you should also have consequences and not show privileges that employees will resent. Remember that accountability starts at the top; you need to set the example.

If you have applied all the solutions you know, and performance still does not improve, then as the boss, you have the ultimate responsibility to exercise the final option: releasing the nonperformer. While this is the most difficult step to take for a manager, by doing it, you will gain the respect of those who stay. They will realize that you are doing what's necessary and fair to the organization. Conversely, by keeping nonperformers on, you are sending a message that you don't take accountability seriously. This will permanently damage the organization, its culture, and you as a leader. Managers responsible for releasing an employee must always remember that as leaders, they are not only responsible for that particular employee but for all employees under their command, and if they fail to eliminate the cancer of the organization, they are damaging the company and—what is worse—losing the respect of their subordinates.

To create more accountability, start by declaring goals publicly and tie them to specific dates for completion. Include not just company's goals but your own goals, and explain how you will hold yourself accountable. Share your plans and action items: who is responsible for what and by when? Emphasize long-term tasks but without neglecting short-term goals. Encourage healthy fighting among workers to explore possible solutions for a given problem. Inspect what you expect; measure progress of each person's action steps, and correct weak situations early and permanently. Remember that not everything that counts can be counted and not everything that can be counted counts. Reward achievements publicly.

Some managers find it difficult to hold remote workers accountable. I am often asked how to keep remote workers accountable. My quick and simple answer is, "The same as with any other worker." However, I know that it can be a challenge to not have employees in view. The secret, as with all employees, is to have clearly defined mutual expectations. What is generally known as an "upfront agreement" or "upfront contract" is a great tool to use for all employees, particularly for remote employees. This contract should include preferred communications method, frequency and details of face-to-face meetings, what the worker needs from the manager to perform to expectations, consequences of not meeting expectations, and of course, very clear instructions, measurements, and expectations. Managers of remote workers must always be available for consultations and to provide the support their workers need. As for reviewing the remote employee's performance, the same methods should be used as for on-site employees, preferable using the goals and objective method explained.

Chapter 6 Takeaways

In teaching accountability, stress the importance of written agreements and determine how they are negotiated.

- Inspect what you expect, and inspect the right things.
- Team members should not hold themselves or others more accountable than you hold yourself.
- It's critically important to hire people who are willing to be accountable.
- Accountability must be pushed to the lowest level in the organization.

- Leaders, and every member of the organization, must never lose sight of the ultimate goal of the company and of the team.
- Instill accountability by giving employees the skills and control needed to respond to tough problems.
- To remove barriers to accountability, start by eliminating practices that undermine it, such as micromanaging and legislating how activities are to be conducted.
- To achieve personal accountability, employees must be allowed to own a project and to answer for the outcome.
- Accountability results from an interlocking system of three elements: clarity, commitment, and consequences.
- Follow the rule, Say what you do, and do what you say.
- Before you consider punishing failures, consider remedies to prevent their repetition.
- To create more accountability, start by declaring goals publicly and tie them to specific dates for completion.
- An upfront agreement or contract is a great tool to use for all employees, particularly remote employees.

CHAPTER SEVEN
OTHER CASES OF ACCOUNTABILITY

How to Evaluate Remote Employees

It is becoming more and more prevalent for companies to have some employees work remotely. The remote location can simply be working from home, or it can be a satellite office many miles away from headquarters. Because of the distance, it can seem impossible to stay on top of what your remote employees are doing on a day-to-day basis. We tend to trust what we can see, which makes it difficult to evaluate employees who aren't in the office. Without regular visual and verbal contact, a large disconnect can grow between team members. Naturally, this raises the question, what can be done to ensure the success of a virtual team while, at the same time, promoting the continued growth and success of the individual and ensuring compliance with the strategies of the company?

Many businesses still revolve around the principle of employees showing up and leaving at fixed hours; these businesses consider punctuality and attendance part of an employee's evaluation program. But when there are virtual teams and management cannot monitor their physical presence, a clear set of evaluation matrices must be established. Managing a virtual team can appear to be less taxing than being physically surrounded by the staff; however, ensuring the success of the virtual team can involve a great amount of effort and organization.

There is no factor more critical than establishing clear expectations; without the luxury of daily interactions, keeping the team motivated and performing well is a challenge. Doing this requires an agreed-upon set of requirements, objectives, and expectations for the work to be done and clear instructions on how each employee is to be measured and evaluated. Naturally, these expectations need to be determined specifically for the circumstances of the team and not only communicated but also agreed to by the employees.

Physical proximity allows for direct employee evaluation; it is often clear when an employee is struggling on a project and needs help, but without the benefit of face-to-face contact, this is more difficult to determine. Frequent checks with the staff are required to monitor their progress, assess their motivation, and determine their overall satisfaction. While this can be fairly time-consuming, it cannot be discounted, and the checks should be regular and often. It's not important whether the employee visits the home office or management visits the remote location (although a combination of the two may be preferred), but what's important is the frequent and organized interaction.

Managing remote staff certainly has its challenges, and therefore, adopting an open and communicative approach is essential to the success of a remote workplace. If you determine the circumstances under which your virtual workers will operate and decide what they are expected to deliver, you will be in a good position to evaluate their performance. A set of easily measurable deliverables must be developed and clearly communicated to the staff. If these criteria are being met and the business goals are achieved, there is a fair chance that the remote arrangement is working.

If people are always in the office early and leave late, others may assume that they are dedicated, hard-working employees, while in reality, they might be less productive than their coworkers. And that's why evaluating remote workers must focus on the actual work itself. Management by objective (MBO) is a recommended approach to evaluate remote workers. As telecommuting becomes more widespread and the workplace becomes increasingly virtual, management by observation simply doesn't work anymore. Supervisors have to concentrate on the what and how of the work, as measured by realistic metrics.

A side benefit of this practice is that by focusing on what work is being done and how it's accomplished, businesses are better able to assess the performance of their employees. As a result, favoritism and office politics generated at the main office are less likely to influence decisions of who is rewarded and who is penalized. And weak links can be identified in real time to receive the additional training and attention they require. Still, it requires a special type of person to be able to work remotely, adapting to a different set of customs and having the concentration and dedication to follow rules even when nobody is watching. Some companies require remote employees to be on camera at all times, using new video communication technologies. This practice is not well received by some people, complaining about the lack of privacy.

While I promote measuring performance by results (ideally using the MBO approach), we must not discount behavior as a component. Since it is possible to achieve results while breaking company policies, employees must be judged on both. Virtual employees who work in physical isolation could easily be tempted to cut corners, and thus managers must figure out ways to evaluate both the performance as well as the behavior of their staff. The natural tendency in the virtual workplace is to rely on various metrics to assess employee performance, but those metrics can lead to counterproductive behavior. For example, call-center workers are evaluated by the average length of their customer calls, but this particular metric can tempt workers to prematurely transfer or terminate calls without really resolving a customer's problem.

My Experience

An engineering VP of a manufacturing firm was valuable to the company because of his technical talents, but he was bad at keeping commitments and meeting goals; in fact, he was retained as an employee only because the company needed his knowledge. His problem was that he wanted to be liked by everyone, and thus, he constantly spent time doing things for others that had nothing to do with his main job. As a last measure before letting him go, the CEO asked me to work with him.

The focus of my coaching had to be making him understand that by tending to menial things for others, he jeopardized not only his job but also the company's success. The process wasn't easy, but after severe therapy, he improved in his accountability, and his performance improved significantly. Because of his improved performance, his peers respected him more, and he became more popular than before.

Since the subject of this book is accountability, we must emphasize that the culture of accountability must be extended to remote working places. This is done by giving responsibilities to remote employees and empowering them to own their tasks or projects; responsibility breeds accountability.

Perfecting Performance Reviews

When doing performance reviews of employees, managers have an opportunity to define and implement accountability. Traditional performance reviews don't really do that because they are typically done to cover a period of time, such as a year, with after-the-fact reviews of performance. That's why I highly recommend performance reviews based on goals and objectives. My book *Performance Reviews: The Bad, the Ugly, the Alternative* discusses the subject in detail and offers an alternative that increases the value of employee performance reviews. With this method, goals are defined between manager and employee for a defined period; the performance is measured by how the goals were achieved (or not). Goals are not unilaterally imposed by management; they are negotiated between the parties. Employees have the opportunity to disagree with the terms or conditions, and because they decide on a de facto contract, they own the project. There is no subjectivity or a different way of looking at things; measurements are clear and without any doubt, and accountability is also clear. This method makes it much easier to implement company-wide accountability, one employee at a time.

MBO is a process of agreeing upon objectives within an organization so that management and employees agree to the objectives and understand what they are. It is a systematic and organized approach that allows management to focus on achievable goals and attain the best possible results from available resources. MBO aims to increase the overall performance of an organization by aligning goals and objectives throughout the organization. The essence of MBO is participative goal setting; management and employees jointly participate in setting the goals, choosing the course of action, and making decisions to reach those goals.

An important part of MBO is measurement: the comparison of the employee's actual performance with the standards set. Ideally, when employees themselves are involved with setting goals and choosing the course of action to follow, they are more likely to fulfill their responsibilities. The principle behind management by objective is to create empowered employees who are clear about their roles and responsibilities, understand the objectives to be achieved, and help achieve organizational as well as personal goals. Empowerment creates motivation; involving employees in the whole process of goal setting increases employee job satisfaction and commitment.

The MBO process, then, is ideal when implementing accountability throughout the organization since it promotes empowerment and the active participation of employees in the development of goals. By providing defined measurements of performance, the MBO system provides a built-in accountability factor; the goals are met or are not, and employees are charged with the accomplishment of the goals they own.

Chapter 7 Takeaways

There is no factor more critical than establishing clear expectations for employees, and without daily interactions, keeping the team motivated and performing well is a challenge.

- Managing remote staff certainly has its challenges.
- Management needs to establish a clear set of evaluation matrices.
- Management by objective is a recommended approach to evaluate remote workers.
- A side benefit of this practice is that businesses are better able to assess the performance of their employees.
- The culture of accountability must be extended to remote workplaces.
- The principle behind management by objective is to create empowered employees.
- The MBO system provides a built-in accountability factor.

CHAPTER EIGHT
EPILOGUE

While establishing and implementing accountability can be seen as the hard side of management, the upside is unlimited. It establishes a culture of trust, openness, interdependence, self-confidence, achievement, appreciation, and energetic celebrations.

One of the greatest motivators for workers at any level is an environment where everyone is heard; people keep their word, are constantly coached to grow in competence and confidence, and enjoy the rewards of accomplishing one success after another. A leader who fosters this will engender deep loyalty and extraordinary commitment.

An added benefit of creating a culture where promises are kept is that it eventually encompasses customers, who believe that the company stands by its products, services, and promises, creating a valuable competitive advantage.

Finally, here are a few other concepts to remember:

- Give people responsibilities, not jobs. To achieve personal accountability, employees must be willing to own a project; personal action must take place to finish the task, and employees must be willing to answer for the results.

- When things go right, praise others; when things don't go according to expectations, assess what you did wrong or determine what you can do to improve the results.
- What you accept is what you teach. If you accept people not meeting deadlines or quality standards, or whatever you expect from a contract that you created with someone to deliver, you are teaching your people that it's okay not to meet that contract.
- The pursuit of mediocrity is almost always successful. Raise the bar. Go for the gold; always aim high. It is better to aim high and miss than to aim low and hit. If you set your goals low enough, you are sure to meet them.

Summary

- Delegating without accountability is just distributing work. No organization can truly succeed without personal accountability.
- Holding people and oneself accountable is the most difficult part of management to be learned; fortunately, it can be learned.
- When employees accept an assignment, they are assuming a contract, and as such, they must abide by the terms of the contract and be held accountable for it.
- Team accountability includes the personal accountability of all its members; if one member fails, the whole team is responsible.
- Accountability starts at the top of the organization; managers must set the example by holding themselves accountable.
- To have accountability, there must be consequences; for example, you need consequences for good performance and consequences for failure to meet the goals agreed to.

Finally, the following list is from John Miller's *QBQ: The Question behind the Question*:

Ten Truths of Personal Accountability

1. Everybody wants everybody else to practice personal accountability.
2. Most people find it easy to make exceptions for themselves when it comes to applying the principle of personal accountability.
3. Excuses are insidious, creeping slowly into our thoughts and language until they become part of our daily living.
4. I am more effective in all roles—manager, colleague, parent, spouse, friend, volunteer—when I practice personal accountability.
5. Personal accountability is a "me" thing, not a team thing. When I practice it, the team can do great things.
6. Personal accountability begins at home, in the family, with outstanding parenting.
7. Life is more fun—and I can be and do so much more—when I walk the high road of personal accountability.
8. Personal accountability is always the better choice over victim or entitlement thinking, complaining, procrastination, and blaming—and expecting others to rescue me from my bad choices.
9. Personal accountability is "trainable"—it can be learned.
10. Asking the right question is always better than asking an incorrect question.

BIBLIOGRAPHY

Albrecht, Karl. *The Pursue of Mediocrity Is Always Successful.*

American Express Open Forum. *Five Tips for Creating More Accountability.* October 2009.

Bloom, Jeremy. *Fueled by Failure: Using Detours and Defeats to Power Progress.*

Cohen, Michael Henry. *What You Accept Is What You Teach: Setting Standards for Employee Accountability.*

Cole, Larry, Cole, Michael, and Baggett, Byrd. *Personal Accountability.*

Collins, Jim. *Good to Great.*

Duncan, Roger Dean. *Avoid the Blame Game: Be Accountable for Accountability.*

Folkman, Joseph. "The 8 Great Accountability Skills for Business Success." *Forbes,* November 14, 2014.

Galindo, Linda. *The 85% Solution: How Personal Accountability Guarantees Success.*

Greiling and Halachmi. *Transparency, E-Government and Accountability.* December 2014.

Koehler, Kathy. *Have You Been Accountable?*

Lencioni, Patrick. *The Five Dysfunctions of a Team.*

Miller, John. *QBQ: The Question behind the Question: Practicing Personal Accountability at Work and in Life.*

Overfield and Kaiser. *One Out of Every Two Managers Is Terrible at Accountability.*

Spector, Robert. *The Nordstrom Way to Customer Service Excellence.*

Stoker, John. *Overcoming Fake Talk.*

Ulrich and Smallwood. *What Is Leadership?*

Viva, Oswald R. *Create a Culture of Empowerment.*
Viva, Oswald R. *Delegate to Succeed.*
Viva, Oswald R. *Performance Reviews: The Bad, the Ugly, the Alternative.*
Wharton, Lawrence E., and Row, Richard. *Accountability: A Little Clarity Please.*

APPENDIX A
WHAT IS ACCOUNTABILITY?

Accountability can be defined as consequences for one's actions or lack thereof. Accountability emphasizes liability for something of value, either contractually or because of one's position of responsibility.

Answer the following questions:

1. Why do you as a leader have great difficulty exercising proper accountability?
    - a culture of conflict avoidance
    - the lack of skills to deal with accountability issues
    - no rewards from above for dealing with accountability
    - all of the above
2. What is your perception of your accountability practices?
3. Are you pushing accountability to the lowest possible level?
4. Are you aware of what needs of yours may compromise accountability?
5. Do you know what you are reinforcing? Are you effectively dealing with it?
6. Indicate true or false for the following statements:
    - Other than holding employees answerable to certain standards of performance and behavior, the next most

desirable level of accountability is from peers, followed next by the supervisor.
- When an outside force (customer, government, etc.) intrudes on the accountability process, a solution is likely to be imposed that may wreak far more havoc than lower levels of accountability would have engendered.
- As one moves from self-accountability to an outside force, less freedom is available to do what needs to be done.
- If leaders do what they say they will do, trust is established, but only if they also control their behavior.
- A leader who is conflict avoider, unreasonable, or abusive to employees probably will not create an environment in which workers feel safe and trust management.
- To remedy an accountability problem, leaders must always start with themselves and realize that they have reinforced the pattern of behavior causing the lack of accountability and therefore are responsible in some ways for what happened.
- To make accountability more productive, leaders must acknowledge, before addressing the staff member's accountability, that they failed to address this issue or did so inadequately.

APPENDIX B
MAKING PEOPLE ACCOUNTABLE

From a white paper in the Alternative Board, contributed by J. Ed Barnes and modified by Oswald Viva.

How to make people accountable. There are basically two approaches to instill accountability in employees; one uses punishment to force people to accept accountability; the other one motivates people to embrace accountability as a way of doing things. The following lists the techniques for each and consequences of them.

1. The punitive approach:

    - Enforce many rules for the completion of the work, including process and methods. Make it hard to stay within them.
    - Apply quotas and penalties if not met.
    - Assume employees know what is expected because of their position or job title. Give incomplete or unclear instructions.
    - Micromanage. Stay on top of employees to make sure they follow instructions or tell them what to do at every step.

Using these techniques will result in people resisting supervision and undermining a supervisor's authority because they don't like being told what and how to do everything. Employees will lose motivation because they will have no ownership in the tasks, and they will put no pride in their work. Tis ultimately results in a lack of accountability.

2. The motivational approach:

- Communicate and sell company vision, making employees participants in it.
- Set and communicate goals and expectations for the business. Deduce goals for employees from the company's goals, and judge them based on achieving those goals.
- Solicit ideas from employees for the goals to be implemented and how to accomplish objectives.
- Reward employees' contributions to the goals and choices of how to achieve them.
- Define individual responsibilities, and negotiate individual goals and what constitute reaching them. Obtain buy-in of negotiated goals.
- Schedule and implement regular reviews of progress, making sure schedules are met by employees and supervisors.
- Investigate reasons for failures, and work out preventative measures to ensure they don't happen again.
- Reinforce training and teaching, prioritizing weaknesses. Apply mentorship for weak links.
- Recognize and reward good progress and achievement of goals. Praise in public whenever possible.
- Promote employees who look for and accept additional responsibilities and reassign those who lack the aptitude for the job (provide them with additional training).

- Remove unqualified employees or those lacking the interest to accept responsibility and accountability. The rest of the team will appreciate not having anchors to their progress.

Using motivational techniques, employees will develop ownership and feel part of the organization's direction. They'll have pride of accomplishment and feel rewarded by their success. They'll feel respected and proud of being part of the organization's success. Ultimately, they will be self-motivated and accountable.

APPENDIX C
DELEGATION

The single greatest cause for failure in managers is their inability to delegate. When we talk about delegation, we must include empowerment and accountability, as these are integral parts of the complete process of delegation. Delegating without empowering people is just distributing work, and delegating without accountability is assigning tasks without expectations.

What Is Delegation?

Delegating is appointing someone else to act on your behalf. "Acting on your behalf" means that you are assigning the authority and responsibility to another person to carry out certain tasks or activities that you usually do.

Effective delegation is the most powerful activity in management because it enables you to direct your focus and energy on those leadership activities that only you can do.

Delegation requires trust in the people you are delegating to, and trust is the highest form of human motivation. Sure, this involves more time than doing the task yourself, but this is time well invested because you are investing not only in the growth and development of an employee but also in the firm and in yourself.

When should you consider delegating? The short answer is,

always, if you want to grow the company and yourself, but particularly when the following is evident:

- When you reach a point in your business where you are juggling too many balls and begin to drop them.
- When you want to free yourself of areas that are not your strengths or you do not enjoy.
- When doing certain functions takes away from doing your job.
- When you have to deal with time management issues.
- When you need to create free time to strategize and plan.
- When you need to reduce the amount of time you are working, not only in hours but days.

You need to delegate to

- create growth in your organization and/or the company,
- protect yourself and the company in case you're incapacitated,
- contribute to the succession plans of the company. You need to delegate as much of your functions as possible in order to create value by covering all positions, and
- reduce stress. If you delegate, you will still be responsible, but you won't have the stress of having to do it all yourself.

You must realize that your staff isn't the source of your problems; they are the solution to them. Don't look at your employees as a time-consuming obligation that you have as manager or leader; if you chose your staff carefully and hired the right people, they should be the help that you need to be effective. Your ability to delegate will make the difference.

How much of your to-do list could you delegate? Dedicate your efforts to identify what you can delegate and determine what you need to have in order to be able to successfully delegate.

What to Delegate

You must select tasks or projects to delegate carefully. In addition to other selection criteria listed elsewhere in this book, you must consider the benefits that you and your organization would obtain from your choices of tasks to delegate. The benefits can be in work time, personal satisfaction, personal or professional development, or life balance.

The following exercise can help you identify those tasks that you can delegate while keeping those you enjoy doing or should continue to do because they are part of your job. It can also help you determine what you need to do or to get to be able to delegate them.

Draw a table with four columns. In the first column, list all the tasks that you do today; in the second column, list those tasks that you enjoy; in the third column, list the tasks that you can delegate today, counting on the people you have, and in the fourth column, list the tasks that you could delegate if you had the right people. (You can also make a fifth column, listing the time that each task should take.)

When completed, it will suggest the alternatives to delegate tasks, keeping those that you want to keep (enjoy), and how much time you would save by delegating, time that you can dedicate to those duties that are critical for your position, to improve yourself, or to balance your life. It will also suggest what you need to do to be able to delegate more.

Use these data to develop a plan to effectively and efficiently establish a delegation process.

> No man will make a great leader who wants to do it all himself, or to get all the credit for doing it.
> —Andrew Carnegie

Delegating Is Difficult

Delegating is the second-most difficult job for a manager or leader to learn, but the good news is that it can be learned. What is the most difficult job, you ask? It is delegating with accountability.

Why is delegating so difficult?

- "Nobody can do it as well as I can." It is probably true that you are the best at doing it, but unless you learn to delegate, you will always be doing that job and not the job you should be doing.
- "I know I should be delegating, but I don't have time to train someone now." Well, guess what? If you don't take the time to train someone to do it, you will be doing it forever.
- Lack of confidence in employees.
- Perhaps the worst reason, and one that people will never admit to, is the reluctance to give up being the expert on certain jobs.
- "Why should I let someone else do it when this is something I truly enjoy doing?"

And even more excuses to avoid delegating:

- Avoidance of change. "If it ain't broke, don't fix it"; however, unless you accept change you, your organization and your company will not grow.
- Concerns about the acceptance of others. You may be afraid that if you delegate, others will perceive you as not wanting to do certain jobs because they are below you.
- Fear that the employee will do it better than you. This reflects insecurity at its maximum.
- Paranoid about sharing your systems or methods.
- You lack the desire to take risks.

- You have a quest for perfection. The right people with the right training should be able to do the job as well as you. Concentrate on hiring right and training thoroughly.

With a culture of not delegating, it will be difficult for a company to expand and grow the business on a profitable basis. Conversely, by practicing effective delegation, you'll give your employees additional job satisfaction, and your organization will be able to utilize the abilities of all its members and channel that energy toward the growth of each member and of the company.

Delegation of responsibility requires equal delegation of authority but not the abdication of responsibility. The person you are delegating to is responsible for completing the task or executing the function properly, but in most cases, you are still ultimately responsible for it.

Delegation Is a Contract

When you are delegating, you are in effect setting a contract with the person you are delegating to. As a contract, it must include rules, expectations, and commitments. The rules are those that you institute to ensure that the task or function will be done right. The expectations are those that you set for the outcome of the task or function.

- The commitments are from both you and the people you are delegating to. Yours is that you will empower them and will provide the tools for them to accomplish the task or function according to your expectations. And the employees commit to dedicating their efforts to meet the objectives and goals of the tasks or function.
- When employees accept the delegation, they assume ownership of the project or task. With ownership come responsibility and the authority to act. By delegating responsibility, you are letting authority flow from you to the employee; however, accountability flows from the employee to you.

- For an effective delegation, employees need to understand why they are doing what they are doing, what results and standards are expected, and how their responsibilities for the task, project, or function fit into the long-term plan of the company. Employees need to know the details and why the task is to be completed, why they were selected to do it, and the conditions for the delegation.
- Identify and transmit your expectations clearly, understanding that expectations are not goals. Communicate the expectations and make sure they were understood by soliciting questions from the person you are delegating to.
- Subordinates must be given guidelines and standards of performance, time schedules to be followed, and rewards/penalties for performance. You need to make sure employees are trained to do the job and know exactly how they expected to perform and what are the rules to follow.
- Subordinates also need
  - a detailed description of the job assigned,
  - a written system or process to be followed,
  - objectives that can be measured; explain how they will be measured, and
  - objectives that are achievable, not impossibilities to test them.

The Delegation Process

Like with most things in business, there must be a system to delegate and a process to follow.

- Identify the need. Make sure you have identified a need to do what you are asking others to do.
- Select the person you will delegate to. *Select* is the key word here; don't just pick whoever is not busy at the moment. Chose employees because their capabilities enable them to perform as needed.

- Plan the delegation. Be sure to cover all the what, when, and how of the job, and be sure you have enough information to transmit to the employee. Retain some control over the project, whether supervisory or for approval.
- Hold a delegation meeting. Whether it is one-on-one or with a team, have a formal delegation get-together in which you explain everything that is involved, and give all the instructions necessary. Give the instructions in writing so there are no misunderstandings later.
- Create a plan of action. Develop a plan with the employee, detailing how the job should be done.
- Review the plan carefully with employees, making sure (double sure) they understand all instructions and the outcomes expected.
- Implement the plan. Once you are comfortable with the delegation and are sure the employee understands, give the green light to start.
- As part of the plan, schedule periodic reviews to check on the progress made. Do not wait until it's too late to make necessary adjustments or repair what is already damaged. It is also important that you keep the dates scheduled, because if you don't, you are sending the message that it is not important.
- Butt out! Yes, once you complete the delegation process, get out of the way and let the employee proceed without your meddling.
- Follow up.
- Follow up.
- Follow up.

I cannot stress enough the importance to check on the progress and compliance of the project; if necessary, make adjustments as you go. If you invade into the area of authority of the subordinate, it will effectively relieve the subordinate from their responsibility.

If you allow this, you will generate confusion, loss of effectiveness, reduced productivity, and loss of morale among the staff.

The formality or informality of the process depends on the size, complexity, and duration of the delegated task or project. For simple tasks delegated to one person, you won't need to do a very formal process, but the basics of the process should still be maintained. The more complex the project, the more detailed the process should be. Use your judgment, but err on the plus side rather than doing a poor job of delegation.

Subordinates should be accountable for the performance of delegated tasks. Evaluate their performance based upon subordinates staying within authority boundaries, as transmitted during the delegation planning.

Causes of Ineffective Delegation

We could name a litany of reasons that make delegation ineffective, but we will concentrate on the most common ones:

- Employees lack the ability. They are not knowledgeable enough about the project delegated or lack the training necessary to perform the task.
- Employees lack incentive. Perhaps the project being delegated was a bad match for their interest and capabilities, or they did not understand why they were chosen or grasp the opportunity for them.
- Employees are unwilling to take risks. This could be because of a lack of motivation or drive, or because of insecurity. If you see some talent in employees that they don't recognize, and you want to help them by giving them this opportunity, tread carefully, and make sure you follow up frequently.
- Employees fear punitive action. They may not feel capable of taking on the responsibility for the project and are concerned that they will be penalized for poor performance.

- Unclear job duties or task assignment. The delegation process was not followed, and you sent the poor employee to a sure losing game, not knowing the rules of the game.
- Constant criticism of task results and techniques. Employees need coaching and encouragement, not negative criticism.
- Lack of achievable goals or defined objectives. The objectives and goals were not clearly defined or were too difficult to achieve.
- And last but not least, keeping control over the employee. When a manager takes away an employee's empowerment, the employee will generally cease performing independently.

As is probably apparent, most of problems are caused by not having properly executed the steps of effective delegation. If any of these problems surface for you, make sure you adhere to those steps, and the problems will likely disappear.

Teaching Delegating to Subordinates

It is not sufficient for you to delegate efficiently and effectively; you must also teach your subordinates to delegate. Delegation should be a company-wide practice if the organization is to be efficient and driven to grow. As it may be difficult for you to delegate, it is also difficult for your employees, particularly if you or the company haven't created the organizational culture that promotes this practice.

Use the process described above to teach your employees to delegate, and continuously encourage them to practice it and improve on it. Monitor progress and correct transgressions or mistakes made, but hold them accountable for the progress (or lack of it) in delegating and achieving successful results of tasks or projects delegated.

"Up Delegation"

This refers to subordinates delegating to the boss. When the boss assigns a task to an employee, and the employee finds a way to get the boss involved in executing the task, it is up-delegating. For example, if employees tell the boss, "I'm not sure what to do next; can you help me?" they are delegating up to the boss to get the boss involved in completing the task. For example, if employees tell the boss, "I can't get the other department to cooperate; can you intervene?" they are delegating up to the boss and demanding action–and time–from the boss.

A task or project typically has two parties involved: one to work it and one to supervise it. As the boss, if you agree to review it, follow it, fix it, or even help on it, you become the owner of the issue. Accepting up-delegation can rob you of critical time that you should dedicate to doing your job rather than what should be the job of your subordinates.

Learn to identify the signs of this convenient way for others to pass the buck back to you, and make the necessary corrections to the delegation process so it will not happen. As you become better at delegating, you won't allow your employees to pass the buck back to you.

The concept of up-delegation is beautifully explained in an article published in *Harvard Business Review* in 1968. The article, "Who's Got the Monkey?" became the most reprinted article in HBR history.

Delegating Criteria

To summarize the subject of delegation, to be successful in delegating, you must accomplish the following:

- You are clear in your delegation, and the chosen employee has demonstrated the capability to successfully take on the project.
- The employee is seeking to take the responsibility. He or she accepts the assignment with enthusiasm and confidence.
- The objectives are clear to everyone involved.
- All the required resources are available. The employee has the tools, resources, and training necessary to be successful.

- You have a high degree of confidence that the project will be successful when carried on by the employee.
- You have clearly specified the consequences of not meeting the objectives.
- You follow up and stay informed on the project's progress and are ready to make adjustments if necessary.

Summary

- When you delegate, you are assigning the authority and responsibility to another person to carry out certain tasks or activities that you usually do. Delegation is the most powerful activity in management because it enables you to direct your focus and energy on the activities that only you can do.
- You need to delegate to create growth in your organization; this protects yourself and the company in case you are incapacitated. This contributes to the succession plans of the company and reduces your stress.
- Delegation is difficult to do when you are not used to it, but it can be learned.
- By delegating, you are establishing a contract with rules, expectations, and commitments. The rules are those that you institute to ensure that the task will be done right. The expectations are those that you set for the outcome of the task.
- There are various levels of delegation, depending on the people involved, the job to be done, and the organization.
- Delegation should be a way of work throughout the organization; thus, you must teach your subordinates to delegate.
- Be vigilant of people up-delegating to you.

www.ingramcontent.com/pod-product-compliance
Lightning Source LLC
Chambersburg PA
CBHW021943170526
45157CB00003B/905